NATIONAL DEFENSE RESEARCH INSTITUTE

WORKFORCE PLANNING

IN THE
INTELLIGENCE COMMUNITY

A Retrospective

CHARLES NEMFAKOS, BERNARD D. ROSTKER, RAYMOND E. CONLEY, STEPHANIE YOUNG,
WILLIAM A. WILLIAMS, JEFFREY ENGSTROM, BARBARA BICKSLER, SARA BETH ELSON,
JOSEPH JENKINS, LIANNE KENNEDY-BOUDALI, DONALD TEMPLE

Prepared for the Office of the Director of National Intelligence
Approved for public release; distribution unlimited

For more information on the RAND Forces and Resources Policy Center, see http://www.rand.org/nsrd/ndri/centers/frp.html or contact the director (contact information is provided on the web page).

For more information on the RAND Intelligence Policy Center, see http://www.rand.org/nsrd/ndri/centers/intel.html or contact the director (contact information is provided on the web page).

Contents

Figures

Tables

Acknowledgments

In the course of this project, we received assistance and insight from many individuals in the Office of the Director of National Intelligence (ODNI) and throughout many elements of the intelligence community. We are grateful to each of them for their time and expertise.

Several individuals deserve special recognition. We wish to acknowledge the guidance of Alex G. Manganaris, director of Workforce Planning and Resources, in the ODNI, Chief Human Capital Office. In particular, his understanding of the base force, gained during his tenure in the Department of Defense during the George H. W. Bush administration, and his appreciation of analyzing risk have been most helpful in supporting our efforts. In addition, several members of his staff, particularly Donna M. Call, currently in the ODNI, and former staff member Belinda LaValle, made important contributions to other segments of this work.

We also wish to thank Dwayne M. Butler and Nelson Lim from RAND and Robert B. Murrett of the Syracuse University Department of Public Administration and International Affairs and formerly director of the National Geospatial-Intelligence Agency for their careful review and comments on earlier drafts of this report.

Abbreviations

AFSC	Air Force specialty code
CEP	Civilian Employment Plan
CHCO	chief human capital officer
CIA	Central Intelligence Agency
DCI	director of central intelligence
DIA	Defense Intelligence Agency
DNI	director of national intelligence
DoD	U.S. Department of Defense
DOPMA	Defense Officer Personnel Management Act
EO	executive order
FY	fiscal year
GAO	U.S. Government Accountability Office
GS	general schedule
IC	intelligence community
IRTPA	Intelligence Reform and Terrorism Prevention Act
IT	information technology
JLDP	Joint Leadership Development Program
MIP	Military Intelligence Program
MOS	military occupational specialty
NGA	National Geospatial-Intelligence Agency

NIP	National Intelligence Program
NIPF	National Intelligence Priorities Framework
NRO	National Reconnaissance Office
NSA	National Security Agency
ODNI	Office of the Director of National Intelligence
OMB	Office of Management and Budget
OPM	Office of Personnel Management
OPMS	Officer Personnel Management System
SES	senior executive service
SME	subject-matter expert
WMD	weapons of mass destruction

CHAPTER ONE

Introduction

Soon after the events of September 11, 2001, the intelligence community began a decade-long effort to reconstitute a workforce that was downsized considerably following the end of the Cold War, resulting in a loss not only of personnel but also of critical capability. Early efforts to rebuild this workforce focused primarily on getting more people on board to respond to growing near-term demands related to the terrorist threat, but these early efforts were haphazard and disconnected. Although the workforce was growing in numbers, there was insufficient visibility into characteristics of the workforce that shape long-term capability, such as the experience distribution; the number of personnel eligible for retirement; the skills and capabilities in residence; and whether these skills were held by civilian, military, or contractor personnel.

Although replenishing the ranks of intelligence professionals was needed, too little attention was paid to the fact that the unique and sensitive nature of the work meant that it could take as long as a decade for young intelligence personnel to gain the skills and experience to become effective analysts. Even experienced candidates who were hired into the workforce needed additional training before they were fully capable.

Before long, the community faced criticism from congressional oversight committees on problems resulting from the rapid and, some might argue, chaotic growth of the intelligence workforce. The establishment, in 2004, of the position of director of national intelligence (DNI), with responsibilities for community-wide personnel policies and programs, created a new opportunity for more-strategic workforce planning within the intelligence community.

The need to make far-reaching changes in a workforce with a wide diversity of elements was challenging, but the chief human capital officer (CHCO) in the Office of the Director of National Intelligence (ODNI) made considerable headway in identifying community-wide workforce issues and identifying tools to facilitate more-effective workforce planning in the future.[1] As the Obama administration enters its

---

[1] In this report, the term *tools* is used in a strategic context—ones that the most-senior managers might use to gain insight into such issues as resource distribution, gaps between workforce demand and supply, and risk.

second term and the potential for budget cuts looms, it is an opportune time to examine the progress made within the intelligence community toward these ends.

This report chronicles intelligence community efforts over more than half a decade to improve community-wide workforce planning and management. Today's resource-constrained environment presents senior leaders with many challenges that require adjustments to both organizational structures and associated resources. The intelligence community leadership bears an additional burden of making these tough decisions without repeating the mistakes that occurred following the end of the Cold War. Within this context, this review provides senior leaders in the intelligence community with an overview of the events leading up to 9/11 as they pertain to the intelligence workforce, and an understanding of efforts to rebuild and manage the intelligence workforce in the decade to come. It also provides perspectives drawn from these experiences and advances general considerations that should be kept in mind as the intelligence community component leaders deal with the consequences of the budget deficit reduction act.

Our report begins in Chapter Two with a discussion of the reforms following 9/11 that motivated a more strategic focus on intelligence workforce planning. In Chapter Three, we move to an overview of strategic workforce planning, highlighting workforce planning tools and concepts that are the central focus of this report. The next two chapters delve into workforce planning tools adopted by the CHCO—those that aid in understanding supply (Chapter Four) and help in forecasting demand (Chapter Five).

The final chapter identifies considerations for the intelligence community as it moves toward a future defined by declining budgets coupled with significant and evolving security challenges. There is little question that this future will require continued adjustment to and reallocation of resources devoted to the intelligence workforce. Even as reductions are made in some areas, investments will need to be made in others in order to sustain and develop needed workforce capabilities as priorities evolve. Thus, the final chapter offers insight to aid the community in protecting the gains made in rebuilding its workforce over the past decade while responding to future challenges.

CHAPTER TWO

Intelligence Community Reform and Workforce Planning

Major intelligence reform after the turn of the century was motivated by a variety of factors: the events of September 11, 2001, and subsequent changes in intelligence priorities; perceived intelligence shortcomings in the lead up to the 2003 Iraq war; and findings of the 9/11 Commission in 2004.[1] These reforms focused on rebuilding and restructuring the intelligence community into a flexible and adaptive organization. The need for greater information sharing among federal, state, and local organizations also took on new emphasis. A central component of this reform was to rebuild the intelligence workforce in order to meet near-term demands associated with the terrorist threat and to develop, over the longer run, a more effective and collaborative workforce that can meet national security challenges well into the future.

This chapter reviews the key events that motivated change in the intelligence community and ties them to the workforce planning efforts that subsequently ensued. The desire to have a well-coordinated intelligence community is not new and can be traced back to the National Security Act of 1947 (Pub. L. 80-253), which established the broad outline for both the intelligence and defense communities. Despite their common roots, the two communities progressed in different ways—the defense community in a more centralized fashion, the intelligence community in a decentralized manner. An appreciation for these different paths is instructive—as is an understanding of how workforce planning has been a tool used by the former, and only recently applied by the latter, as a means of exercising control.

Intelligence Community Rebuilding

The failure of the intelligence community to detect and prevent the tragedy of September 11, 2001, is well documented in the 9/11 Commission report. The report

---

[1] Formally established in late 2002 as the National Commission on Terrorist Attacks Upon the United States, the 9/11 Commission was chartered to prepare a full and complete account of the circumstances surrounding the September 11, 2001, terrorist attacks, including preparedness for and the immediate response to the attacks. See National Commission on Terrorist Attacks Upon the United States, 2004.

highlights the twin problems of the post–Cold War drawdown of personnel and capabilities and the long-festering problems of a fractionated community. The size of the intelligence workforce began declining as the Cold War ended with the fall of the Soviet Union—reflecting the apparent elimination of the most serious threat to U.S. national security. Workforce reductions were implemented by eliminating positions, imposing hiring freezes, and attrition. Within this context, the intelligence community was radically downsized, resulting in a decrease in core capability—a trend that continued until the September 11 attacks.

After the events of 9/11 and beginning in fiscal year (FY) 2002, the agencies of the community were authorized to hire new personnel—reversing the decade-long decline in employment levels that started with the end of the Cold War. The effect is illustrated in Figure 2.1, which reflects both the loss of numbers and loss of expertise.[2] Years of little or no hiring, followed by years of rapid hiring, resulted in a workforce dominated by senior and junior personnel, with shortfalls in the midcareer workforce. Although this workforce distribution is not uncommon in federal government agencies that have experienced similar cutbacks followed by rapid hiring growth, it is particularly challenging in organizations, such as intelligence community components, in which it takes a long time to train individuals to a high standard—an average of ten years for an intelligence analyst.

Figure 2.1
Experience Distribution of Intelligence Community Workforce in One Agency, 2007

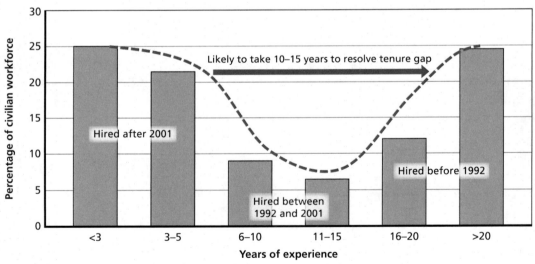

SOURCE: Manganaris, 2010, p. 4.
RAND RR114-2.1

---

[2] This figure reflects data from a single intelligence agency as of July 2007 but is representative of the community writ large during that period.

The 9/11 Commission report identified failures of imagination, policy, capabilities, and management across the government. With respect to the intelligence community, specifically, the commission stated, "The combination of an overwhelming number of priorities, flat budgets, an outmoded structure, and bureaucratic rivalries resulted in an insufficient response to this new challenge [the threat of Islamist terrorism]" (9/11 Commission, 2004, p. 12). With respect to community-wide management, the 9/11 Commission found that the director of central intelligence (DCI) as head of the Central Intelligence Agency (CIA), coordinator of the intelligence community, and "intelligence analyst-in-chief to the president," had "too many jobs" to provide effective leadership. The commission recommended establishing a national intelligence director who would oversee the national intelligence centers and "oversee the agencies that contribute to the national intelligence program, a task that includes setting common standards for personnel and information" (9/11 Commission, 2004, p. 33).

The Intelligence Reform and Terrorism Prevention Act (IRTPA) of 2004 (Pub. L. 108-458) was the response to the 9/11 Commission's recommendation to provide stronger leadership in the intelligence community. The act established the position and office of the DNI—the position first filled by John Negroponte. Although the aim of this measure was to improve coordination across the intelligence community, achieving the goal would be much easier said than done. The sprawling and diverse nature of the community, with widely varying institutional missions and cultures, as well as a lack of centralized control of resources, has proven exceptionally difficult to harmonize—despite the need.

Elements of the community report to various agency heads, work within different personnel and budgeting authorities, and report to different congressional committees. Although the new law addressed some of these challenges, the DNI was given broad responsibility but more-ambiguous authority—a result of the fact that many elements of the community are embedded within other cabinet departments and overall authority is in the hands of the cabinet secretaries. At the time, the U.S. Government Accountability Office (GAO) also noted, "Human capital considerations, such as the recruitment and retention of key skills and competencies, performance incentives to share information, and more flexible approaches to the management of human capital, are crucial to the success of the intelligence community reforms" (Mihm, 2004, p. 18).

A year after Congress passed the 2004 legislation, the WMD Commission echoed the need for fundamental change in the intelligence community.[3] Among its recom-

---

3   *WMD* is an abbreviation for *weapons of mass destruction*.

Formally established on February 6, 2004, by Executive Order (EO) 13328, as the Commission on the Intelligence Capabilities of the United States Regarding Weapons of Mass Destruction, the commission was charged with assessing

whether the Intelligence Community is sufficiently authorized, organized, equipped, trained, and resourced to identify and warn in a timely manner of, and to support United States Government efforts to respond to, the development and transfer of knowledge, expertise, technologies, materials, and resources associated with mendations, the commission called for the community to "build a modern workforce" and noted the substantial personnel authorities granted to the DNI (WMD Commission, 2005, p. 19). The WMD Commission recognized the difficulty within the community of "recruiting and retaining individuals with critically important skill sets—such as technical and scientific expertise, and facility with foreign languages" and noted that the community "has not adapted well to the diverse cultures and settings in which today's intelligence experts must operate" (WMD Commission, 2005, p. 20). The commission proposed creation of a new human resources authority in the ODNI "to develop Community-wide personnel policies and overcome these systemic shortcomings" (WMD Commission, 2005, p. 20). The position of CHCO was created shortly after the ODNI was established.[4] The commission also offered "specific proposals aimed at encouraging 'joint' assignments between intelligence agencies, improving job training at all stages of an intelligence professional's career, and building a better personnel incentive structure" (WMD Commission, 2005, p. 20).

Concurrently, in 2005, the Senate Select Committee on Intelligence initiated an audit of personnel growth in the intelligence workforce. The purpose of the audit was to review activities and resources necessary to support projected personnel growth from 2006 to 2011, as well as underlying requirements for additional personnel. Although the committee was sympathetic to the aggressive post-9/11 campaign to increase the size of the intelligence workforce to support the war on terrorism, it was concerned about the uncontrolled nature of the growth and significant shortcomings in the state of the workforce. In its 2007 report, the committee identified issues and inadequacies in the following areas: understanding of the number, cost, and use of contractors; infrastructure needs (such as office space) for new personnel; capacity in training facilities; hiring lead times and practices; language proficiency; the growing seniority of the workforce; and mentoring the large percentage of the workforce hired after 9/11.[5]

In addition, EO 12333, "United States Intelligence Activities" (Reagan, 1981), as amended by EO 13470 (Bush, 2008) sought to strengthen the role of the DNI. The objective was to help create a more effective intelligence community, in which the agencies could better integrate, work more collaboratively with one another, and more freely share information. The amendment updated EO 12333 to conform to the new intelligence structures and the intelligence reform law passed in 2004, to reflect the roles and responsibilities of the DNI, and to provide implementing guidelines for some of the recommendations from the 9/11 and WMD commissions. Section 1.3 delineates

---

the proliferation of Weapons of Mass Destruction, related means of delivery, and other related threats of the 21st Century and their employment by foreign powers (including terrorists, terrorist organizations, and private networks . . .). (Bush, 2004, § 2[a])

[4] The CHCO is in charge of human resource strategy issues and policies for all U.S. intelligence organizations and is responsible for overseeing the implementation of the personnel provisions of the IRTPA.

[5] Senate Select Committee on Intelligence Audit of Intelligence Community Personnel Growth, not available to the public.

24 provisions in which the DNI is told that he or she "shall" or "may," depending on the topic, undertake certain activities. Section 1.3(d) addresses the DNI's authorities with respect to appointments and removals of senior intelligence community officials. By and large, with respect to selection of senior community officials, the order replicates the language in the 2004 IRTPA. However, it also gives the DNI a voice in the removal, when that proves to be necessary, of senior intelligence officials. Additionally, this provision addresses the position of the Under Secretary of Defense for Intelligence, which was not referred to in the IRTPA.

Role of the Director of National Intelligence in Workforce Planning

As head of the intelligence community, the DNI has wide-ranging responsibilities, including the development of personnel policies and programs to enhance the capacity for joint operations and to facilitate staffing of community management functions.[6] In establishing the position of DNI, the 2004 IRTPA states,

> The Director of National Intelligence shall prescribe, in consultation with the heads of other agencies or elements of the intelligence community, and the heads of their respective departments, personnel policies and programs applicable to the intelligence community that—
>
> (i) encourage and facilitate assignments and details of personnel to national intelligence centers, and between elements of the intelligence community;
>
> (ii) set standards for education, training, and career development of personnel of the intelligence community;
>
> (iii) encourage and facilitate the recruitment and retention by the intelligence community of highly qualified individuals for the effective conduct of intelligence activities;
>
> (iv) ensure that the personnel of the intelligence community are sufficiently diverse for purposes of the collection and analysis of intelligence through the recruitment and training of women, minorities, and individuals with diverse ethnic, cultural, and linguistic backgrounds;

---

[6] Although the act specifies these responsibilities, it also states that each agency head is responsible for managing his or her own agency. For stand-alone agencies that are totally dedicated to intelligence, the ultimate responsibility for managing the agency's resources is with the agency head. However, most of the intelligence agencies are embedded within other departments, and the overall responsibility is with their department heads. So, although the act specifies considerable responsibilities, this dichotomy undercuts the authority of the DNI.

(v) make service in more than one element of the intelligence community a condition of promotion to such positions within the intelligence community as the Director shall specify; and

(vi) ensure the effective management of intelligence community personnel who are responsible for intelligence community-wide matters. (Pub. L. 108-458, 2004, § 102A)

The emphasis on people as a critical part of the needed reforms was reinforced in numerous community guidance documents. The 2005 *National Intelligence Strategy* highlighted the importance of human capital transformation, stating among its enterprise objectives the need to "[a]ttract, engage, and unify an innovative and results-focused Intelligence Community workforce" (ODNI, 2005, p. 13). The strategy elaborates that the community must "recruit exceptional individuals from a diverse talent pool, train and develop them to meet the challenges they will face, and then deploy them in ways that maximize their talents and potential"; "reward expertise, excellence, and commitment to service"; and "build an Intelligence Community–wide culture that values the abilities of each of its members" (ODNI, 2005, pp. 13–14).

Publication in June 2006 of the *US Intelligence Community's Five Year Strategic Human Capital Plan* further underscored the importance of the intelligence workforce (ODNI, 2006). In its foreword, the DNI, John D. Negroponte, wrote,

There is no doubt that the success of the U.S. Intelligence Community in helping preserve the nation's security depends above all on the dedicated military and civilian members of our workforce. . . . This Five Year Strategic Human Capital Plan will underpin the IC's [intelligence community's] ongoing transformation. It is designed to bring more community-wide coherence and cohesion than ever before to the way IC agencies lead and manage their people. (ODNI, 2006, p. iii)

The plan established three broad goals: to develop an agile, all-source workforce; to win the war for talent; and to create a culture of leadership at all levels of the workforce.

The intent of the IRTPA was to give the DNI authorities that were unavailable to the DCI: authorities over budgets, civilian personnel, and infrastructure. But executing these formal authorities, even as they pertain to personnel policies and strategic workforce planning, has proved problematic. A comparison with the "national military establishment," also created by the National Security Act of 1947 (Pub. L. 80-253), is instructive in understanding why building a strong DNI has been so challenging.

Parallels in the Evolutions of the Defense and Intelligence Structures

Following World War II, the National Security Act of 1947 set the foundation upon which both the military and intelligence bureaucracies were built. Following a common paradigm, the act created multiple coordinating organizations, but, for a time at least, a confederation of existing independent and powerful agencies were largely left free to exercise previously held prerogatives. As initially established, the positions of Secretary of Defense and the DCI were thought of as coordinating positions. The Secretary of Defense was to coordinate the activities of the national military establishment, which consisted of the Departments of the Army and Navy; the DCI was to coordinate the intelligence that was produced by the Departments of State, the Army, and the Navy. Yet from this common starting point, these positions and their corresponding organizations developed along very different paths.

The defense establishment was the first to centralize power starting in 1949, with the establishment of the Secretary of Defense as a cabinet-level position, the subordination of the Departments of the Army and Navy as units of the U.S. Department of Defense (DoD), and the creation of the Department of the Air Force. After DoD was established, a series of reforms and initiatives during the 1950s concentrated power in the Office of the Secretary of Defense. Congress also underwent its own organizational reform, merging the separate Military Affairs and Naval Affairs Committees of both houses into a single Armed Services Committee in each chamber; there would be a single Defense Appropriation Committee in each chamber as well.

Importantly, in establishing the Secretary of Defense position, the 1949 and subsequent amendments to the National Security Act addressed the issue of control over resources, giving the secretary's office responsibility for overseeing a uniformed budget and system of accounts for the military departments. Control over the budget and over apportionment of appropriated funds within the department greatly increased the secretary's power—power that was skillfully used by Robert McNamara when he became Secretary of Defense in 1961. McNamara developed the decision support tools that underpinned his efforts to "rationalize the defense program"—to fulfill the secretary's responsibility for shaping the defense program in the national interest. This analytic focus transformed the defense budget from a bookkeeping device to a mechanism for integrating strategy, forces, and costs.

Among the tools that helped rationalize the defense program were (1) the five-year defense plan, which projected forces, manpower, and costs into the future; (2) the draft presidential memorandum, which highlighted issues in a structured process; (3) the Systems Analysis Office, which applied the techniques of rational decisionmaking to the problems of national defense; and (4) the Military Manpower Requirements Report, which documented numbers of people needed to meet the department's mission in three broad categories—mission forces, general support activities, and personnel support activities. These basic tools have been expanded and strengthened over the years to the systems in place today. In addition, the Goldwater-Nichols reforms of 1986 further centralized control by empowering the Chairman of the Joint Chiefs of Staff to resolve requirement issues among the military services.

In contrast, the intelligence community developed in a very different way, remaining largely decentralized. An important difference between the defense and intelligence establishments is the fact that the Secretary of Defense gained budgetary and management authority, whereas the DCI never did. And without such authority, the DCI had little power to exercise his or her role in intelligence coordination. Furthermore, early on, as the CIA became the locus for covert action, the DCI was diverted from a coordination role as manager of the overall intelligence community. The 2004 act sought to address some of these problems—aiming to bring more-centralized control into the ODNI and enhancing the authorities of the director's position. Borrowing from the experience of the defense department suggests that incorporating analytic tools in workforce planning in the intelligence community could serve to strengthen integration.

Workforce Planning in Intelligence Community Integration

Many observers have noted that effective workforce planning is key to implementing intelligence reform.[7] In 2007, Ronald Sanders, the intelligence community's CHCO, stated, "Here is the challenge that the Intelligence Reform and Terrorism Prevention Act gave us: The DNI does not have chain-of-command authority over the intelligence agencies . . . as a general proposition, he can't tell them what to do" (Pourinski, 2007). As a consequence, Sanders believed that the ODNI has to "take a far more collaborative approach." Effective workforce planning could be a key element in such a strategy. Shortly after taking over as DNI, Michael McConnell talked about creating a "'culture of collaboration'—between staffs of the different agencies." "I believe if we can incentivize collaboration, drive collaboration, cause individuals in one organization to serve in a different organization, and reward that behavior, I think we will get to this," he told reporters (Waterman, 2007). Integral to success was the DNI's ability to leverage personnel powers.

As described above, congressional committees charged with overseeing intelligence affairs also understood the importance of workforce planning and put pressure on intelligence community members to systematically look at identifying and satisfying workforce requirements. In the Senate Select Committee on Intelligence's report on the Intelligence Authorization Act for Fiscal Year 2008 (U.S. Senate, 2007), the committee charged the DNI with assessing the number of people employed in each agency of the intelligence community and providing that assessment to Congress.[8] The

---

[7]   See, for example, Vivian, 2003.

[8]   Although the Intelligence Authorization Act for Fiscal Year 2008 was vetoed, the request for personnel-level assessments informed the formation of the Civilian Employment Plans (CEPs) and contractor accounting that is described in Chapter Four.

assessment was to include three parts: (1) basic personnel and contractor information; (2) justification for requested funding levels; and (3) an evaluation of the funding levels to ensure adequacy in providing the needed infrastructure, training, and administrative and operational support for the requested personnel and contractors. The DNI and the community were also charged with developing a plan that tied all parts of the personnel system together.

Workforce planning can be a means not only of improving the performance of individual agencies within the community but also of supporting better integration of the community as a whole, leading to greater productivity. In the 2006 strategic human capital plan, the DNI stated, "Nothing could better serve the goal of integration, acting as a powerful force for bringing cohesion to the Community and its various components and employees" than a more strategic approach to the intelligence workforce (ODNI, 2006, p. 35).

In the main, the focus of the DNI's authorities is on resource-allocation decisions. In the intelligence community, one of the most important resources is its people. If the ODNI is to execute its resource-allocation authorities, it needs to establish structures that will have an impact on workforce planning decisions. In point of fact, the CHCO has proved to be the most aggressive element of the ODNI in pursuing cohesive and coherent personnel policies.

CHAPTER THREE

Strategic Workforce Planning

The essence of workforce planning is ensuring that the right people with the right skills are in the right place at the right time to meet an organization's goals. Workforce planning is a systematic process of identifying, acquiring, developing, and retaining employees to meet the needs of an organization.[1] The "strategic" element denotes the integration between workforce planning and an organization's strategic plan—its mission, goals, and objectives—thus aligning organizational priorities with the budget and human resources necessary to accomplish them. In short, it draws attention to the "people factor."

The benefits of workforce planning are many. It provides a strategic basis for decisionmaking while allowing for flexibility in an evolving environment. It enables an organization to anticipate workforce needs rather than react to surprises, both in the short and long terms. It can involve contingency planning for potential future circumstances and consider options that mitigate risk. It provides a better understanding of the areas of the workforce that need to be strengthened or pruned and, in doing so, facilitates the development of plans for staffing levels, succession planning, and skill development. Workforce planning creates a connection between mission, strategic plans, and human resource needs that maximizes operational effectiveness.

The ODNI has adopted the strategic workforce-planning model depicted in Figure 3.1.[2] The first steps in this process are fundamental building blocks for all government agencies. The entire process encompasses five steps:

1. **Strategic assessment** links workforce planning to an organization's mission, goals, and objectives. The aim is to identify and document organizational strategic factors that will affect strategic workforce planning. Activities include

---

[1] In the previous chapter, we referred to *manpower* and *personnel planning*, terms typically used within DoD to refer to the demand for and supply of people. Today, the terms *workforce planning* and *human capital planning* are used more frequently to refer to demand for and supply of personnel, as well as potential gaps or surplus in capability that may result from an imbalance in demand and supply.

[2] The ODNI process described here is a derivative of the process for strategic workforce planning provided by the Office of Personnel Management (OPM). Although there are several approaches to conducting a workforce analysis, there is little substantive variance from the OPM methodology (OPM, undated).

environmental scans, internal and external research, leadership insights, the organization's business strategy, and workforce composition. The outcomes are organization strategic direction, external and internal human capital drivers, and a future vision with broad human capital goals.

2. **Gather and analyze supply and demand data.** This step involves gathering existing and projected workforce information required to support the mission. More specifically, this means the following:

   a. *Understanding supply* involves analyzing the present workforce in terms of numbers, competencies, job classification, salary, location, education, retirement eligibility, and other relevant characteristics. This assessment should include not only a snapshot of the current workforce profile but also trend

Figure 3.1
Office of the Director of National Intelligence Strategic Workforce Planning

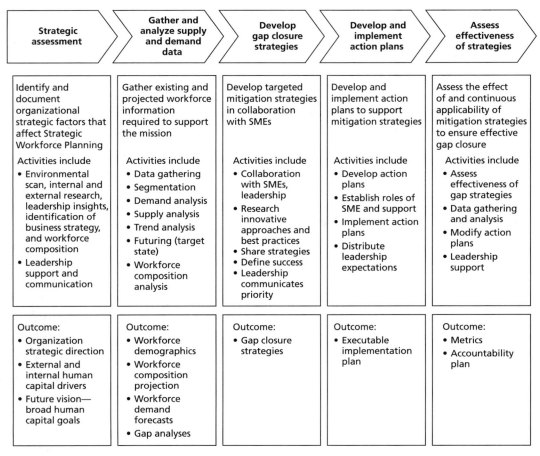

SOURCE: ODNI.
NOTE: SME = subject-matter expert.
RAND RR114-3.1

analysis, such as the turnover rate, how long it takes to fill positions, and whether turnover is concentrated in certain skill sets.

b. *Forecasting demand* centers on analyzing the staffing levels and competencies needed to carry out the organization's mission. This step considers not only what work will be done in the future but also how it will be done, identifying anticipated changes in such areas as mission, budget, skills and competencies, and technological advancements. It then determines how these changes will affect the workforce—type of work, staffing levels and competencies, development needs, and other workforce-related effects.

3. **Develop gap closure strategies.** Once supply and demand are understood, workforce gaps become evident. This step involves developing targeted mitigation strategies in collaboration with subject-area experts. Activities include collaborating with experts and organizational leaders, researching innovative approaches and best practices, sharing strategies, defining success, and engaging leadership in communicating priorities.

4. **Develop and implement action plans.** This next step involves developing and implementing action plans to support mitigation strategies. Here, activities include developing action plans, determining how they will be carried out, and implementation. In carrying out these plans, it is essential to ensure that leadership expectations are well understood.

5. **Assess effectiveness of strategies.** The final step is assessment—assessing the impact and continuous applicability of mitigation strategies to ensure that gaps have been effectively closed. An organization will need to revisit the tasks in the second step, gathering and analyzing supply and demand data as appropriate, and modify plans accordingly.

Workforce planning is not a one-time effort. It must be revised and updated on a periodic basis to incorporate changes in organizational strategy and priorities, as well as outside factors, such as enabling technologies, that affect the workforce.

The remainder of this report focuses on the second step in the process, gathering and analyzing supply and demand data. As mentioned in the previous chapter, gaining a better understanding of the rapid growth of the intelligence workforce after 9/11 was of particular interest to the oversight committees—with criticisms centered less on the need for rebuilding and more on understanding how much of what capabilities were needed and what component of the workforce was best positioned to fill the requirements.

Workforce Planning in the Intelligence Community

Since 2006, the ODNI has sharpened its focus on strategic workforce planning from a community-wide perspective. The ODNI's CHCO during much of this period, Ronald Sanders, employed an array of tools and concepts to advance workforce planning. Some of these tools aim to improve data-collection capabilities: to simply understand the size and characteristics of the community's workforce within and across its various departments and agencies. Other tools focus on improving the community's capability to forecast workforce demand: to connect the intelligence mission to the number and type of personnel needed to accomplish the mission, and to evaluate risk in resource allocation. With these capabilities, the connection between existing workforce capabilities and future requirements becomes clearer and enables better-informed decisions about hiring and retention—about where capabilities need to be expanded or where they can be cut.

The next two chapters provide an overview of these tools and concepts. Chapter Four examines tools that focus on understanding supply: civilian employment plans, the Joint Duty Program, a framework to account for core contractors, and considerations associated with the military workforce. Chapter Five looks at tools that facilitate demand forecasting: workforce demand forecasting methods, a methodology for aligning resources with national priorities, and the base force concept. Before turning to a discussion of these tools, we briefly examine characteristics of the intelligence workforce that are of consequence in the context of workforce planning.

Characteristics of the Intelligence Workforce

The U.S. intelligence community is made up of 17 member agencies that are diverse in nature. Two broad characteristics of these agencies have relevance to the task of workforce planning: One is the organizational structure of the community, and the second is the composition of the workforce.

Though commonalities exist across all agencies, the structures of these agencies vary and fall into three broad categories. One group consists of agencies whose sole mission is intelligence. This group includes the CIA, National Security Agency (NSA), National Geospatial-Intelligence Agency (NGA), National Reconnaissance Office (NRO), and the Defense Intelligence Agency (DIA).[3] The second group consists of agencies with a significant intelligence component that organizationally are part of a larger agency that has other missions in addition to intelligence, and part of their intel-

---

[3] The CIA is the only stand-alone agency in the intelligence community. The other agencies whose sole mission is intelligence—NSA, NGA, NRO, and DIA—are components of DoD; as such, their authorities are split between the agency head, the Under Secretaries of Defense for Personnel and Readiness and Intelligence, and the DNI.

ligence capacity is organized to support those other missions. The agencies with large embedded intelligence offices include the Federal Bureau of Investigation; the Departments of the Army, Navy (including both the Navy and Marine Corps intelligence elements), and Air Force; and the U.S. Coast Guard.

The last group consists of agencies with a small intelligence component within a larger agency with other missions. These components generally represent a specialized niche of interest to the broader intelligence community and national security officials. They include the Department of State, Drug Enforcement Administration, Department of the Treasury, Department of Energy, and the Department of Homeland Security. The 17th member agency is the ODNI. These organizational differences can greatly affect agency-specific approaches to workforce planning. They also affect the ability of the ODNI to harmonize workforce planning across the community, as well as identify relevant issues or concerns.

A second characteristic of the intelligence workforce that has a significant impact on workforce planning is its composition—that it has government civilian personnel (27 percent), military personnel (54 percent), and contractors (estimated at 18 percent).[4] Each personnel category brings unique capabilities and strengths, an understanding of which is important in determining their optimal use in meeting mission goals and objectives across the community and within each member agency. Ideally, the individual components of the workforce should be developed and managed to ensure that they complement each other and that their unique capabilities are leveraged to enhance the overall effectiveness of the workforce.

As discussed in the next two chapters, the CHCO has sought to improve workforce planning in the intelligence community by providing tools that will enable better utilization of available supply, as well as aid in demand forecasting and risk mitigation.

---

[4]   Figures are approximate.

CHAPTER FOUR

Understanding Supply

The previous chapter laid out a five-step process for workforce planning. This chapter focuses on the supply component of workforce planning, part of the second step in that process. The intelligence workforce consists of civilian, contractor, and military personnel. Tools that not only account for the size of these components but also aid in establishing an appropriate balance among them provide value to senior leaders. In this chapter, we offer an overview of workforce planning tools used by the CHCO to improve understanding of the community workforce. It covers the Civilian Employment Plan; the Joint Duty Program, a tool to increase workforce flexibility; a framework to account for core contractors; and workforce planning as it pertains to the military workforce.

In the particular context of this review, while wartime supplemental funding lessened financial pressures, constraints on the size of the civilian workforce and military end strength complicated arriving at solutions—in some cases, leading to the use of contractor personnel in roles that might have preferably been assigned to government employees. Additionally, wartime priorities constrained access to military personnel. These circumstances underscored the importance of using the type of tools described here to better understand the characteristics of the intelligence workforce community-wide.

Civilian Employment Plan

The Civilian Employment Plan (CEP) was the first community-wide workforce planning tool put into effect by the DNI. The 2007 Senate Select Committee on Intelligence report outlined concerns that the intelligence community lacked an integrated plan for achieving and sustaining projected civilian personnel growth. In response, the ODNI used the Civilian Employment Oversight Board to assist agencies in developing agency-specific CEPs that align with strategic and operational guidance issued to the agencies. In this regard, RAND was asked to help structure the CEPs and work with individual agencies as they developed their own plans.

The methodology used to construct the CEPs was mandated by then-CHCO Ronald Sanders and motivated by questions and concerns raised by the congressional oversight committees. The CHCO's aim was to underscore the community's progress in responding to congressional concerns through improvements in processes and practices that would lead to effective workforce planning and development.

Agency Plans

The CEP provides a snapshot of the workforce mix and projected future requirements for each agency, as well as various aspects of workforce planning. It describes efforts to rebuild the numerical strength of the civilian workforce, making up about 27 percent of the workforce community-wide—highlighting an agency's strength and growth areas. Though the plans have evolved over time, the initial CEPs contained four sections that remain at the heart of the plans today: agency overview and strategic link, human capital requirements, current workforce profile and composition, and major human capital initiatives. In reality, the CEPs go beyond understanding supply and, for the civilian workforce, provide estimates of future requirements, as well as initiatives under way that aim at mitigating gaps.

The **agency overview** provides background information, including history, origin, and laws establishing the agency. It includes the agency's mission and intelligence mandate, as well as its responsibilities and regulatory functions. It also includes an overview of the agency's organizational structure and how it fits into the intelligence community. This information provides crucial context because the differences among the elements within the community necessarily lead to varying approaches to workforce planning.

The second section details **human capital requirements**. Human capital, or workforce, requirements are projected over the budget planning period. Identifying future requirements helps ensure that personnel are in place and trained to meet foreseeable needs. Requirements must consider the number of personnel, the correct mix of skills and analytic capabilities to complete the agency's mission, and what sector of the workforce can best meet expected needs—civilian, military, or contractor. Because threats can rapidly change, forecasting requirements must incorporate some element of flexibility so agencies can respond quickly to changing threat environments.

The third section, current **workforce profile and composition**, captures the characteristics of an agency's workforce, which includes its current workforce and the resources available to them. As context, this section begins with a description of the specific nature of the work performed at the agency and how the workforce is distributed across different roles. The size and type of support provided by contractors is also included. The demographic profile of the agency is presented, along with information about how the agency is encouraging diversity in the workforce and the strategies employed. This section contains not only static information on the current workforce and its composition but also data on how the workforce has changed since the prior fiscal year in terms of funding, percentage of positions filled, and other significant changes, as well as information on how workforce problems are being resolved. Career training programs are described as well. Figure 4.1 illustrates some of the data presented.[1]

The final section describes major **human capital initiatives**, identifying strategies for closing gaps in skills and capabilities—recruitment and retention strategies and plans and other workforce initiatives that are reflected in the upcoming president's budget. Finally, critical supporting infrastructure is discussed, identifying investments the agency is making that affect workforce accomplishments described in the CEP, an example of which is training.

There have been proposals for expanding the CEP to include additional information. For example, a fifth section on the base force was recommended for addition to the CEPs after this concept was introduced by the CHCO. The intent of this section was to describe how the agency's workforce is broadly linked to intelligence priorities, as well as the processes an agency has in place to reallocate personnel to meet changing priorities. In addition to linking the workforce to intelligence priorities, this section would also provide visibility into how the workforce is distributed between direct mission support and general, enterprise support—which differs based on whether an agency has centralized or decentralized support activities.

In essence, as workforce planning tools and concepts expanded, the results of these efforts could be folded into the DNI's CEP instructions.

Community-Wide Civilian Employment Plan

Following preparation of the first agency CEPs, a community-wide CEP was written that, in effect, presented an integrated strategy for the civilian workforce across the intelligence community. It served as a mechanism for the DNI to identify the most-pressing issues concerning the civilian workforce across the community and propose opportunities for collaboration in identifying solutions. Integrating each agency's CEP into a community-wide plan was a challenging effort because of the diversity of organizations within the community, as described in Chapter Three, and their individual agency-led approaches to workforce planning. The task required more than simply adding up the numbers from the individual plans. Because the CHCO recognized the complexity and difficulty of creating an integrated story, he asked RAND to help develop the community-wide report as part of the annual budget submission.

The use of contractors serves as an example of the diversity within the elements of the intelligence community. The agency CEPs clearly illustrated the increase in the use of contractors, which was originally considered a short-term solution to capability shortfalls in the workforce, and described plans for reducing the relative size of the contractor force over the coming years. But the picture in each CEP differed

---

[1] Notional data are presented in this figure because actual numbers are not available to the public.

Figure 4.1
Notional Data Included in Civilian Employment Plans

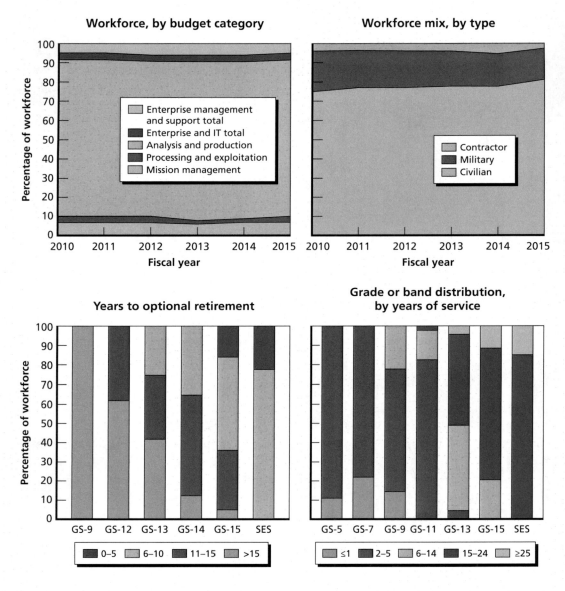

NOTE: IT = information technology. GS = general schedule. SES = senior executive service.
RAND RR114-4.1

by type of organization. Large numbers of contractors tended to be more prevalent in the intelligence-only agencies, in which the workforce is already focused full time on intelligence-related problems and there was less built-in surge capability—likely because of Cold War–era cutbacks. In contrast, embedded organizations could draw on resources from other parts of the organization to help fill immediate and short-term needs, and therefore made less use of the contractor workforce.

These early agency CEPs also helped focus attention beyond the numerical aspects of the workforce, to requirements associated with maintaining the correct mix of skills and analytic capabilities to complete an agency's mission. If skills and experience are lost or declining in critical areas, awareness of these changes motivates development of alternative staffing strategies to mitigate risk of personnel shortfalls when significant lead time is needed for workforce development. Perhaps the best illustration of this is where CEPs highlighted foreign-language capabilities as an area in need of significant growth.

In the aggregate, these early CEPs provided insight into workforce trends that the community needed to address. One is the number of retirement-eligible employees. The loss of senior employees is difficult to combat rapidly because they hold a great deal of institutional knowledge and experience that take time to develop over the course of a career. Hiring new employees or promoting junior employees more rapidly does not necessarily solve this problem; instead, individuals may simply be placed in senior positions before they are ready—creating an entirely different challenge.

The dearth of midcareer employees was another characteristic of the intelligence workforce highlighted by the agency CEPs. A shortage of midcareer employees may portend a future leadership gap in parts of the community, or gaps in the transfer of knowledge between senior and junior employees. With such trends illuminated in a community-wide CEP, the community and individual agencies have an opportunity to put mitigating programs in place—such as continuity-of-leadership efforts that create a structure for mentoring junior employees so that wisdom and experience are more systematically passed on to the next generation of analysts.

A community-wide CEP may also highlight commonalities and differences in the type of workforce initiatives under way throughout the intelligence community. In general, agencies have developed specific initiatives to ensure that they will have the best mix of analysts, managers, supporting employees, training programs, IT resources, and building space. However, demands placed on embedded agencies differ from those placed on dedicated intelligence agencies. Embedded agencies, particularly the relative newcomers to the intelligence mission, are grappling with how to incorporate new intelligence functions into organizations that have traditionally focused on different missions. These agencies must also determine how to staff their intelligence functions when current employee pools are trained for more-traditional missions. Thus, their recruiting, training, and infrastructure initiatives must be tailored for these unique circumstances. Initiatives common across the community include expanding the workforce, improving personnel retention, enhancing training programs, preparing for a lack of managerial personnel, and fostering community-wide collaboration.

Joint Duty Program

As described previously, the final section of the CEP describes major human capital initiatives. One such initiative is the Joint Duty Program, which served as a tool to both expand workforce flexibility and provide for professional growth. The IRTPA included a provision requiring the DNI to prescribe "mechanisms to facilitate the rotation of the Intelligence Community personnel in the course of their careers in order to facilitate the widest possible understanding" of the range of intelligence requirements, methods, users, and capabilities through the community (Pub. L. 108-458, 2004, § 102A). Such a program can increase workforce flexibility by creating a pool of individuals with broader understanding of intelligence operations beyond a single element—effectively expanding the capability of a portion of the workforce. This pool of individuals becomes a useful resource in workforce planning.

The concept of the intelligence Joint Duty Program was patterned after the Goldwater-Nichols Department of Defense Reorganization Act of 1986 (Pub. L. 99-433), which requires "joint" assignments for uniformed officers before they advance in rank. According to the 2004 intelligence reform act, the DNI, in consultation with the member-agency heads, was to prescribe personnel policies and programs to do the following:

- Encourage and facilitate assignments and details of personnel to national intelligence centers and between elements of the intelligence community.
- Set standards for education, training, and career development of personnel within the intelligence community.
- Make service in more than one element of the intelligence community a condition of promotion to such positions within the community as the DNI specifies.

In 2006, the DNI issued a directive for the Joint Duty Program, followed in 2007 with policy guidance that prescribed requirements for obtaining joint duty credit. Individuals rotate to joint duty positions for at least 12 months and for no more than 36 months, without obtaining an exemption. Under policy guidance, participating individuals can receive joint duty credit for working in another intelligence community element, in the ODNI or one of its components, within a home agency in a position that has been specifically designated as joint duty, in certain liaison and equivalent positions or on internal assignments (such as serving on joint task forces), or in an organization outside the intelligence community. An individual deployed to a designated combat zone for 179 days or more satisfies the 12-month requirement for joint duty credit.

The civilian Joint Duty Program was called out in the *500 Day Plan* (ODNI, 2007), issued in October 2007, as a core initiative in the community's aims to create a culture of collaboration—the first focus area described in the plan. As stated in the report,

The Joint Duty program provides rotational opportunities for civilian IC professionals, as a prerequisite for senior rank. As part of this initiative, a companion Joint Leadership Development Program (JLDP) is designed, developed, and begins to deliver and reinforce Joint Duty experiences. It also ensures that senior leaders gain a Community-wide focus, as opposed to an agency-centric focus. (ODNI, 2007, p. 5)

The program develops an "IC professional/leadership corps that has strong inter-agency experiences and information sharing relationships, allowing the IC to quickly identify and leverage unique skills and insights from across the IC and bring them to bear against complex threats" (ODNI, 2007, p. 5).

Since the inception of the program in May 2006, the ODNI has identified hundreds of senior executive positions in the intelligence community that will require joint duty as a prerequisite, and it has opened an interagency website that lists hundreds of joint duty placements for community civilian personnel. In 2008, the program received the Innovations in American Government Award in recognition of its success in promoting cross-collaboration and knowledge sharing between federal intelligence agencies (Ballenstedt, 2008).

According to a 2012 GAO report evaluating the Joint Duty Program, "IC officials cited enhanced collaboration, increased networking, and a better understanding of the community as a whole as positive aspects of the Joint Duty Program" (GAO, 2012, p. 10). The program is widely supported across the community (currently, all elements except the Coast Guard participate) and benefits individuals and agencies alike. For program participants, it offers a new opportunity for professional development, and agencies gain as returning personnel leverage their new skills.

Accounting for Core Contractors

The intelligence community will always have a need to supplement its government workforce with core contractors (about 18 percent of the community's workforce) who bring particular experience and expertise, as well as offer surge capability in periods of extreme demand, as was the case after 9/11.[2] But striking a balance among civilian, military, and contractor personnel is critical to sustaining a healthy operational environment, in which each component of the workforce is used to its comparative advantage.

---

[2] This discussion examines core contractor personnel who augment U.S. government civilian and military personnel by providing direct technical, managerial, or administrative support to intelligence community elements. They are typically integrated in the community workforce and perform staff-like work. Core contractors are distinct from independent or industrial contractors who are contracted to provide specific goods or services. This distinction is identified in ODNI, 2009.

Following the attacks of September 11, 2001, demand grew rapidly for broader and deeper intelligence activities, products, and services. As the intelligence workforce had sharply declined over the previous decade, hiring contractors was a way to rapidly increase capacity to meet growing demands. Further, contractor support, hired for a limited and defined period of performance, was better suited to the supplemental funding that was largely paying for the war against terrorism than long-term commitments to government civilian employees.

Although contractors provided immediate surge capacity, their growth in the intelligence workforce was considerable and outpaced mechanisms to track that growth and ensure that contractors were being used properly. Core contractors often replaced government workers or filled new requirements that, traditionally or by law, would have been filled by government personnel. Some were assigned responsibilities that many argue should have been reserved for government employees. It was these circumstances that motivated a 2005 audit of the intelligence workforce by the Senate Select Committee on Intelligence. The committee identified the lack of accountability for the use of core contractors as a major concern. Issues raised by the committee included the *proper role and mix* of core contractors, as well as *associated costs*—which had been estimated to be about 30 percent more than those costs for similar government civilian employees.

Managing Core Contractor Inventory

In response to congressional criticisms, the ODNI took action to more closely manage the core contractor inventory, culminating in changes in how the community tracks and defines core contractors, as well as how they are distributed across program areas. A particular aim was to reduce reliance on core contractors and ensure that they are not performing inherently governmental activities.[3]

As a first step, the ODNI initiated an inventory of the contractor workforce—a step well in line with addressing congressional concerns to "provide an accurate accounting of their contractors." Without a basic understanding of the number, quality, and use of contractors in the intelligence workforce, it would not be possible to establish better oversight mechanisms and management controls. The Office of Management and Budget (OMB) developed the initial data-collection template, used in FYs 2007 and 2008, the aim of which was to take a "snapshot" of core contractor presence in the intelligence workforce. The data collected captured best estimates of funding sources, contractor data, and type of work for all contractors funded by either the National Intelligence Program (NIP) or the Military Intelligence Program (MIP).

Initial data-collection efforts were confounded by many factors, not the least of which was the lack of a common definition of what constituted a core contractor—prompting OMB to establish an official definition. Core contractors

---

[3] OMB Circular A-76 prohibits core contractors from engaging in inherently governmental work (OMB, 2003).

provide direct support to core IC mission areas such as collection activities and operations (both technical and human intelligence), intelligence analysis and production, basic and applied technology research and development, acquisition and program management, and/or management and administrative support to those functions. (Kennedy, 2006, p. 1)

Other issues included incongruent definitions of occupational categories among community elements; reluctance to share data because of issues of covertness; and a lack of common understanding of the data elements, such as what constituted a full-time equivalent. Further, underreporting was a pernicious issue largely because of differences in definitional approaches. As these issues emerged, official core contractor numbers showed an artificial increase—a problem that was eventually resolved.

To impose a level of consistency on the process, the Contractor Inventory Working Group was established to develop working definitions and adjudicate issues that emerged. Initial data-collection and analysis efforts pointed to useful refinements in the data element template that would result in improvements in the information collected. An expanded set of data elements was used in FY 2009, the "base year" for managing the core contractor workforce, and continues to be used today.

The results of the inventory also motivated the ODNI to establish a formal policy for integrating core contractor personnel into the intelligence workforce based on mission requirements and comprehensive workforce planning—motivation echoed by OMB's call for agencies to "adopt a framework for planning and managing the multi-sector workforce that is built on strong strategic human capital planning" (Orszag, 2009).

On October 30, 2009, ADM Dennis Blair, then DNI, issued Intelligence Community Directive 612 (ODNI, 2009), which outlined appropriate uses of core contractor personnel as follows:

- to provide support for an immediate surge
- to accomplish a discrete, nonrecurring task
- to provide unique expertise
- to provide a specified service
- to overcome insufficient staffing resources
- to transfer institutional knowledge
- to provide support when the use of a contractor is more efficient or effective (ODNI, 2009, pp. 1–2).

This directive gave the intelligence community a specific policy by which to identify appropriate use of core contractors and better balance the total workforce. Consistently with this policy, the community elements have analyzed their reliance on core contractors and identified positions that could be converted to government employees. Those conversions are under way, though it will take years to complete. The NSA, for example, developed plans to convert several hundred government positions over the FY 2011–2015 time frame.

Further refinements to the data-collection elements have been proposed that will standardize the concept of "full-time equivalent" and capture a more comprehensive view of contractor effort community-wide. A benefit of this refinement is that contractor effort can be better tracked over time to determine whether levels of contractors in total, and relative to the civilian and military workforce, reflect policies for total workforce mix.

Military Workforce

The military workforce is the largest single source of personnel that staff positions throughout the intelligence community. Active-duty military from the four armed services—Army, Navy, Air Force, and Marine Corps—make up just over half of the total community workforce. Military personnel bring unique assets to the community workforce, providing capabilities that complement the other workforce components. Thus, understanding the military workforce and its contribution not only in number but in capability is critical to determining the optimum mix of military, civilian, and contractor personnel to meet mission requirements. As stated in the strategic human capital plan, "better planning and utilization of military members . . . including comprehensive career management, [can] improve the return on our investment in their hiring and training. This will require close collaboration with the military services" (ODNI, 2006, p. 11).

The DNI is responsible for directing and overseeing the NIP, in which a significant number of military personnel are employed. The NIP includes the CIA Program, National Reconnaissance Program, Consolidated Cryptologic Program, General Defense Intelligence Program, and the National Geospatial-Intelligence Program. Most military personnel are employed in the MIP of the military departments and are used to acquire intelligence for the planning and conduct of tactical operations. The MIP is directed and controlled by the Secretary of Defense. In general, the MIP has more junior and company-grade officers and enlisted personnel than the NIP, which has more senior personnel. Military personnel in the intelligence career field can expect to serve in both NIP and MIP positions.

As military personnel flow between their respective services, the combatant commands, and the intelligence agencies, they bring existing skills, knowledge, and abilities, and they acquire new ones that help enhance the overall performance of the intelligence community. Military personnel bring their expertise to intelligence assignments, which, in turn, leads to improved products for military operations. Likewise, the combatant commanders and services benefit from having military personnel who understand the national intelligence capabilities and can translate them to appropriate forces.

Workforce Planning Goals Apply to the Military Workforce

The intelligence community strategic workforce planning goals and objectives are equally applicable to the military component of the workforce as to others. But applying these goals to the relatively rigid military career structure can present challenges, as we describe in the remainder of this section. Furthermore, intelligence personnel practices vary among the military services, requiring tailored solutions in managing the military workforce.

Develop the Individual

Military personnel bring diverse and essential talents to the intelligence mission. Most of these individuals will spend a short period of their careers in intelligence organizations, though some may serve the majority of their careers in intelligence assignments. Overall, the number of military personnel assigned to fill positions in the intelligence community declined considerably between FY 2000 and FY 2008, as requirements of combat operations in Iraq and Afghanistan took priority. Shortfalls in military personnel present a challenge for the intelligence agencies that must fill the empty positions with personnel drawn from the civilian and contractor workforce. The fill rate has improved somewhat over the past few years, but, as the Army and Marine Corps downsize, the availability of military personnel may not substantially increase, and shortfalls could persist. To ensure that this trend reverses over the longer term, the community must provide challenging and engaging assignments that contribute to professional development. And the military services must assign higher priority to filling intelligence positions with talented professionals.

Facilitate Integration

Synchronizing the workforce across the spectrum of intelligence missions requires that the intelligence agencies and the military services seamlessly integrate intelligence positions into planned military career paths. One component of such integration is to better inform military members about intelligence career paths. But equally important is the need for greater clarity regarding current and planned demand for and supply of personnel across the spectrum of intelligence missions—identifying the specific skill requirements in key intelligence occupations, which may differ for the various elements within the community. Important as well is determining which positions are optimally filled with military personnel.

Optimize Workforce Investment

Resource decisions must provide the best value to support the mission, which, in part, translates into the need for greater workforce agility: working more intelligently, more quickly, and more efficiently. The intelligence community has to continually assess requirements and determine the optimal mix of civilians, military, and core contractors to meet national priorities. Workforce agility can be achieved by ease of personnel movement across organizations and by greater speed in developing new workforce skills and competencies.

Challenges in Managing the Military Workforce

Although there is mutual gain from military personnel serving in the intelligence agencies, the organizations in this complex web have different priorities and different approaches to personnel development. The military services recruit, train, employ, and develop uniformed members for a variety of missions, including intelligence missions. The intelligence agencies then utilize uniformed members at varying stages of their military career.

One challenge, alluded to previously, is the declining availability of military personnel in the intelligence field. Intelligence agencies and the military services will need to work together to validate military requirements, making realistic estimates of how many military positions can be filled. The military services have processes for incorporating intelligence requirements into their planning and budgeting systems and for identifying personnel to fill these authorizations; they also have training systems to meet changing demands. But military personnel may also have other qualifications and specialties that compete with assignments to the intelligence community. The services need to incorporate the appropriate personnel flow into development and assignment plans, and fill intelligence positions reserved for military personnel. In turn, the intelligence community must ensure that the positions to which military personnel are assigned truly take advantage of the unique qualities and expertise that military personnel can offer and that they are not positions that could be filled by civilians with military experience or insight from a joint assignment.

Another challenge involves the career structure in the military services, which is not optimal in a career field, such as intelligence, in which it can take five to ten years to develop a fully capable professional. Furthermore, military careers can be relatively short when compared with the civilian workforce because of the pace of career progression and relatively early retirement. The military personnel system is an "in-at-the-bottom, up-through-the-ranks" system. In practice, entry is at zero years of service, with a large percentage of officers retiring at 20 years of service and the majority of enlisted members leaving far sooner. Lateral entry into the midcareer ranks is uncommon. Therefore, increasing the size of the force generally means increasing accessions or retention. And although the latter raises the experience level in the ranks, which is ideal in the intelligence career field, higher retention cannot be the solution to all requirements.

Military intelligence careers are less robust than nonintelligence careers. Members in the intelligence field typically leave well before their colleagues in other occupations, depriving the intelligence community of the talent it needs.[4] Restructuring career opportunities is possible using flexibilities built into existing personnel management policies for both officers and enlisted personnel that would provide incentives for longer tenure in the intelligence career field.

Summary

Regular analysis of the intelligence workforce—civilian, contractor, and military—in terms of numbers, competencies, retirement eligibility, and the many other characteristics discussed in this chapter are a necessary foundation for effective workforce planning. Many of the concerns identified by the Senate Select Committee on Intelligence in 2007 focused on the need for the intelligence community to better understand the characteristics of the intelligence workforce—the number, cost, use of contractors, proficiencies, and the growing seniority of the workforce, for example. The tools discussed in this chapter, and employed by the CHCO, were aimed at addressing these concerns. Without an understanding of workforce supply, both at a given point in time and how these trends change over time, it is not possible to identify shortfalls and overages in the workforce. To do so, however, requires not only information on supply but also the ability to forecast workforce requirements—the demand component of workforce planning, which is the subject of the following chapter.

---

[4] The appendix provides an analysis of the status of military personnel in intelligence and nonintelligence career fields.

CHAPTER FIVE

Forecasting Demand

The previous chapter described the supply component of workforce planning as it pertains to the various components of the intelligence community workforce. Another major element of strategic workforce planning, as established in Chapter Three, is forecasting future demand for personnel. Forecasting demand is often a more challenging aspect of workforce planning because it requires organizations to look into the future and determine how changes in missions and organizational priorities might require adjustments in personnel. Various tools are available to aid in forecasting demand, not all of which are applicable to every element of the intelligence community. This chapter examines three different approaches to identifying requirements: workforce demand forecasting methods, aligning resources with national priorities, and the base force concept.

Workforce Demand Forecasting Methods

The CEPs were a vehicle to ensure consistency between annual DNI strategic guidance and workforce planning. But the process of drafting the first CEPs brought to light the fact that many elements of the intelligence community lacked the internal processes to conduct true workforce planning—particularly the processes needed to forecast future requirements. And, where internal processes did exist, they were not aligned across the community. Thus, the ODNI turned to RAND to define a more systematic approach to forecasting demand for particular skills and experience and to identify tools that can support such planning activities throughout the intelligence community. In response to this request, RAND conducted a workforce requirement workshop in May 2009, the principal purpose of which was to present an approach to forecasting workforce demand that explicitly ties requirements to national intelligence priorities. The suite of tools described later in this section can be tailored as appropriate for all community elements.

Linking Priorities to Workforce Requirements

Workforce requirements must be based on a set of priorities from which intermediate objectives, tasks, and their associated capabilities can be derived. Figure 5.1 illustrates the formal path of how these requirements and priorities flow into the intelligence community through the ODNI (left side) and into the individual intelligence elements (right side). In the intelligence community, initial guidance comes from the White House in the National Security Strategy. From this strategy, the National Intelligence Strategy is constructed and reflected in the National Intelligence Priorities Framework (NIPF). The priorities in the NIPF provide program guidance and help give weight to national intelligence execution tasks across the various agencies in the community, which, in turn, derive individual requirements based on their mission (Figure 5.1, left side).

Figure 5.1
Planning Hierarchy

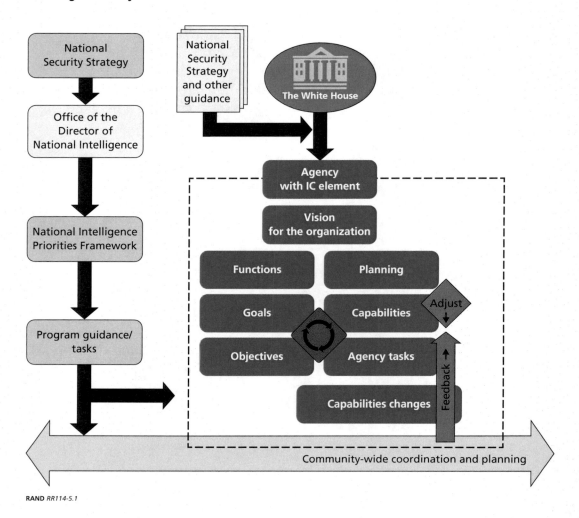

The guidance, as described above, is communicated to each element of the intelligence community (Figure 5.1, right side). Individual agencies, which may have all or only part of their functions associated with intelligence, evaluate this guidance idiosyncratically against the vision for their organization. The agencies conduct their own internal planning to determine what capabilities are needed to respond to the guidance, what exists, and where additional resources are needed. The illustration shows how various levels of information relate to the internal processes. As guidance changes, agencies must reevaluate their capabilities and make changes in response. Planning functions occur not only within each community element but also across agencies, reflecting the community-wide planning lens of the ODNI.

Deliberate planning that starts with priorities, as stated in the National Intelligence Strategy, provides a highly visible means for organizing information about workforce capabilities and for forecasting future needs. It allows decisionmakers to review the strategic and operational effects of decisions in a rational and deliberate way. If mission and support requirements for personnel are based on a set of assumptions as articulated in strategic guidance, they are intuitively persuasive to external audiences and stakeholders: Lower-level objectives are linked to national strategy in a clearly defined hierarchy, and justifications for resource decisions are established. Further, it is easier to justify and defend requirements as budget trade-offs are made and to link workforce changes to needed infrastructure. Deliberate planning also enables managers to anticipate change rather than simply react to unanticipated events.

A structured approach, as depicted in Figure 5.2, helps make workforce requirements more explicit and aids decisionmakers in building a balanced program. As the figure shows, strategic guidance and the tasks, priorities, and relationships implied in that guidance, including both long- and short-term investments, are system drivers that determine the resources needed for organizations to conduct their primary missions— collection, management, exploitation, and the like. In turn, the primary mission drives both primary support requirements and general support requirements—that is, the personnel, facilities, and support requirements, including education, training, technology, infrastructure, and human resources. Collectively, these demands drive total workforce requirements that will be filled by civilian, military, and core contractor personnel, optimally balanced to make best use of each element's comparative advantage and training.

As we worked through this process with intelligence community elements, it became evident that, as is the case with many organizations, clearer criteria existed for determining workforce requirements to achieve the organization's *primary* missions but far less so for *support* functions. Common support functions in the federal government include financial management, human resource management, facilities management, education and training, logistics, IT management, science and technology research and development, and legal services. As the intelligence community reallocates personnel to meet changing mission priorities or executes planned changes

Figure 5.2
Structured Approach to Developing Workforce Requirements

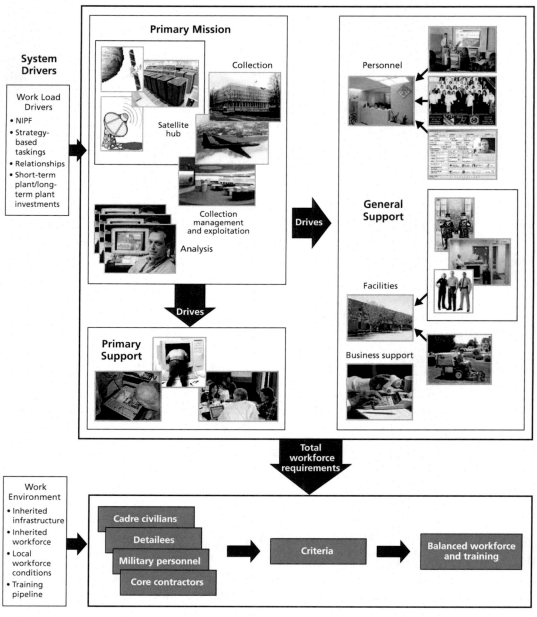

RAND *RR114-5.2*

in processes, it must maintain an appropriate balance in support functions and processes as well. The forecasting methodologies described in the next section can be used by the intelligence community to help identify workforce requirements for both mission and support functions according to strategic priorities.

Forecasting Models and Methodologies

Forecasting methodologies involve measuring workloads and activities, estimating the required workforce size, and describing the skill sets or competencies needed in the future. When selecting an approach, an organization must consider its size, how it is organized, and how programs are managed and budgeted. The scope of impact is another relevant criterion, which, in the intelligence community, could mean the mission of an individual agency, a component within an agency, or community-wide impact. As the scope increases, so do the data collection and analysis involved in forecasting future requirements, as well as the time and effort to conduct the analysis. We briefly describe three common approaches that increase in complexity with each level.

Level 1: Baseline Data Analysis

Level 1 involves data-based analyses that identify relationships between staffing patterns and historical workloads, which, in turn, become the basis for developing a baseline staffing level. These techniques are useful in determining the cost of incremental staffing changes, by providing insight into basic workforce activities and the associated human resource cost drivers. A baseline data analysis can also be useful in identifying where more-detailed and elaborate assessments are warranted. The benefits of these limited analyses include minimal time to assess requirements and minimal direct involvement by people in the various work areas. A key drawback is the lack of cost data for specific processes or an ability to compare process costs for alternative requirements.

Level 2: Subject-Area Expert Workshops

Level 2 methodologies augment level 1 techniques with more-extensive data collection and measurement plus workshops with subject-area experts. The more-expansive process-level data collection provides human resource costs broken down by major processes. The added depth has the following benefits: Reliable data are available for prioritizing and selecting which processes should be improved; the data are useful for comparing process costs when doing comparative analysis and benchmarking with other organizations; and the added depth lays the groundwork for future workforce requirements. These benefits, however, must be balanced against the added cost and time required to conduct more in-depth assessments—costs and time that may not be appropriate for every case.

Level 3: Detailed Work Measurement and Advanced Modeling

Level 3 methodologies make even more-extensive use of personnel and require significant subject-area expert involvement through workshops, detailed measurement, and data collection. Although these techniques provide the most-accurate workforce estimates, they are also the most time- and cost-intensive. Level 3 techniques are normally reserved for processes that are important to the mission, consume most of the resources, and, therefore, warrant the more extensive effort to collect and analyze data.

The approach selected by an organization or component should be based on the level of detail needed to achieve its goals, data requirements, accuracy needs, and timeliness. All functions or work centers do not lend themselves to the same method of determining requirements. A reasonable expectation would be to use the least expensive approach that will produce acceptably valid and representative data within the shortest time.

Aligning Resources with National Priorities

As workforce planning efforts continued, the need for a mechanism to communicate national security priorities to the intelligence community became evident. This need motivated the decision to use the NIPF, which is the primary mechanism through which the DNI captures national intelligence priorities and communicates these issues to the community for action. The DNI uses the NIPF to ensure that strategic guidance shapes long-term initiatives and that the allocation of intelligence community resources is driven by mission priorities.

The NIPF consists of intelligence topics approved by the president, a process for assigning priorities to countries and nonstate actors with respect to each of those topics, and a matrix that reports priorities by topic area for each actor. It is accompanied by written guidance to the community explaining critical information needs associated with the priorities in the matrix. The NIPF was designed to be updated on at least a semiannual basis, though this has not always happened. The community leadership uses the NIPF to guide and inform decisions concerning the allocation of collection and analytic resources and to prioritize collection requirements.[1]

In its current form, however, the NIPF presents limitations for resource decisionmakers and managers facing relatively long planning horizons. First, the NIPF provides only generic guidance on the relative priorities among civilian intelligence collection and analysis needs. Second, it provides this guidance in terms of a snapshot of intelligence priorities—so it is a static measure at a single point in time. Yearly changes in the NIPF could result in very wide swings in priorities, resulting in instability in programs as managers try to keep up with the latest changes. The NIPF does not include information on the relative stability of priorities across topics and actors between iterations of the NIPF, nor does it address the likelihood that priorities have changed or may change in future iterations. Finally, the size of the framework means that it has thousands of individual values, making it difficult to organize or identify groups of priorities.

---

[1]   This discussion of the NIPF draws from an Office of the Director of National Intelligence document that is not available to the public.

Hedging Against Uncertainty

Community managers who use only the most recent NIPF as the basis for resource decisions are forced to react to requirements at a single point in time and may miss influential trends. Analysis on how priorities change over time would enhance decisions regarding future personnel and infrastructure requirements and potentially provide the needed lead time to develop mitigating strategies in cases in which priorities might change on short notice. It can also lead to savings in resources that might otherwise be wasted in a more reactive, short-term decision environment. Thus, tools that help senior leaders *anticipate change and hedge against uncertainty* as they forecast requirements and make resource-allocation decisions have tremendous value.

RAND researchers developed a tool, called the uncertainty tool, that incorporates a methodology to help decisionmakers understand the risks associated with allocating intelligence resources when the lead time required to develop these capabilities exceeds the decision horizon. Figure 5.3 illustrates how this approach fits into the intelligence community's resource-allocation processes. In general, the approach highlights the degree of change, or volatility, associated with intelligence priorities over time and predicts the likelihood of continued volatility.

The methodology uses a data warehouse in which data from the NIPF are gathered and structured for analysis and an analytical tool—the uncertainty tool—that is used with the data. The tool creates information that is objective and reproducible and that takes into account relative risk. Although decisionmakers will still need to use considerable judgment in determining strategies for dealing with risk, they can make more-informed decisions in balancing resources across the portfolio of intelligence programs. The outcome is resource-allocation strategies that hedge against risk and that are informed, substantiated, transparent, and replicable—whether steady state, a focused allocation strategy to increase resources, or a hedging strategy.

Figure 5.3
Dealing with Risk in Developing Resource-Allocation Strategies

The approach assumes that successive versions of the NIPF reflect changing priorities. Some actors, particularly nonstate actors, disappear, reappear, or appear for the first time in any given version of the NIPF. This volatility may create uncertainty in how to successfully plan for future changes. This methodology captures these trends—identifying not only levels in priority associated with a particular state or issue but also changes in the priority over time. This approach helps managers understand whether certain priorities are likely to be long lasting and stable over time or are more likely to fluctuate, especially in more-recent periods.

The analytic approach in the uncertainty tool was derived from risk assessment and volatility measurement concepts in the financial world.[2] Although specific analytic methods from the financial sector were not applied to the NIPF, the methodology developed captures three characteristics of those methods: (1) the long-term relative importance of a priority over time; (2) the magnitude and direction of change in a priority from one point in time to another (in this model, this is the change in priority of a state or issue between versions of the NIPF); and (3) the variation in a priority over time. With this information in hand, decisionmakers can view trends and gain a longer-term view of shifts in intelligence priorities.

The methodology uses data from all existing NIPFs to assess persistence and change over time for particular actors and issues.[3] The tool can be used to perform three main types of analysis:

- **Trend analysis.** A basic use of the tool is to identify trends for particular actors or groups of actors, issues, or their intersection—highlighting patterns that might otherwise not be apparent. A decisionmaker can quickly see where volatility is high for a given topic or see periodic "flare-ups" for an issue with respect to a particular country and whether these flare-ups have recurred or are a one-off phenomenon.
- **Forecasting and weighting.** Another use is as an aid to forecasting whether resources allocated to a given topic area or a particular country need to be maintained, expanded, or reduced. Because past events often provide good predictors for future events, volatility rankings can help illuminate whether resource levels need to be adjusted. A user can adjust what priorities to emphasize—for example,

---

[2]   The Chicago Board Options Exchange's Volatility Index, for example, is an index for understanding stock market volatility by providing portfolio managers with a measure of expected short market volatility. It also provides an index to aid in writing future options contracts.

[3]   Previously, it was not possible to access all NIPF data because of the way those data were presented in each release of the NIPF. RAND researchers created a database in which all NIPF data are stored in a "data warehouse" and available for analysis. As each NIPF is released, the new information will be added. Currently, a Microsoft Excel spreadsheet houses the data; it is hoped that, in the future, this spreadsheet will be converted to a relational database to provide flexibility and enhance sophistication of the calculations and presentation of results.

placing more emphasis on priorities assigned in more-recent versions of the NIPF or assigning more weight to a particular administration's priorities. Assessing such alternatives can provide further insight into how volatile particular issues have been or how they have changed over time.

- **Hedging.** Hedging involves the use of charting techniques to compare and contrast issues and actors. This technique helps inform decisionmakers in cases in which mitigation strategies may be required to meet long-term requirements or in which a capability may take years to develop, spanning many versions of the NIPF. A hedging strategy is particularly useful in assessments involving a group of actors or topics that have high volatility compared with other groups. For example, knowledge that a given actor has been associated with a high level of volatility over many versions of the NIPF provides a useful context if, for example, more-recent versions of the NIPF suddenly assign a low priority to this actor. In such circumstances, it may be prudent to maintain a baseline capability rather than make drastic reductions.

What each of these analyses has in common is the perspective gained from assessing trends in intelligence priorities, based on those established in a series of NIPFs, rather than making decisions based on a single point in time. The tool's results give decisionmakers insight into what to pay attention to: the actors and issues with the highest level of volatility, particularly those for which both significance and volatility have consistently been high. Results affirm states of continued interest to the intelligence community in which sustained emphasis is called for and highlight the unexpected and a potential need to rebalance resource levels. In essence, it sorts areas of high volatility from those that are understood with greater certainty.

By separating priority and volatility, it is possible to identify actors or regions with high priority over time, suggesting a continued, steady-state focus, as compared with actors or regions with high volatility, which suggests the potential need for hedging strategies to ensure that needed capacity can be attained within a reasonable cost and time. Areas with relatively high scores in both priority and volatility suggest both sustained focus and flexibility for the future.

Perspective on how priorities change over time; the ability to compute and compare outcomes based on different assumptions; and the ability to forecast volatility with respect to actors, issues, or regions offer decisionmakers a means of incorporating risk and uncertainty into resource-allocation decisions using data from the NIPF. It enables less-reactive and more-deliberate decisionmaking in an uncertain environment. Although this methodology was developed primarily to support workforce planning, it can be used to inform other resource-allocation decisions as well, given that the NIPF was created to align broad collection and analysis priorities.

Base Force Concept

Another tool that can be used in forecasting demand is the *base force concept*, which offers a baseline from which to extrapolate requirements that result from priority changes and risks. The base force concept was first articulated in DoD to manage force reductions at the end of the Cold War—a period of declining defense budgets and rapidly changing strategic context, not unlike the environment faced by the national security establishment today. Its applicability to workforce planning in the intelligence community stems from the ODNI's desire for a mechanism by which to ensure that workforce capabilities gained following 9/11 are not lost as budgets decline, as was the case in the decade following the end of the Cold War. The base force concept offered just such a tool.

Evolution of the Base Force in the Department of Defense

In 1991, DoD released the Base Force Review, led by Chairman of the Joint Chiefs of Staff Colin Powell. The review responded to dual influences on the department. First, the dynamic post–Cold War strategic environment, dominated by the dissolution of the Soviet Union, called for broad rethinking of U.S. roles and missions after decades of orientation toward deterring a nuclear-armed superpower. Second, increased concern in the late 1980s and early 1990s about rising federal deficits and a sluggish economy became an impetus for deficit-battling legislation. Amid calls for a "peace dividend," the defense department became an attractive potential bill payer.

From this review, the "base force" emerged as a concept to simultaneously orient DoD to future strategic challenges and to manage the reduction in force structure to meet future threats, by establishing a lower limit on the size and shape of the force. Powell's experience with the post-Vietnam drawdown reportedly made him sensitive to the dangers of downsizing too quickly or too haphazardly. Thus the base force provided a structure for proactively managing inevitable force reductions without stripping away too much desired capability or undermining important investments. From Powell's perspective, the base force defined the minimum necessary force to defend and promote U.S. interests (GAO, 1993).

The base force evolved from the August 1989 National Military Strategy that reflected the changing strategic environment. It emphasized forward presence, planning for regional conflict, and crisis response. It also reflected priorities set in the George H. W. Bush administration's August 1990 defense strategy that emphasized a reorientation away from deterring Soviet aggression and coercion and toward preparedness to meet regional threats. Equally, it considered how to meet these requirements at a time of downward pressure on the defense budget.

The base force methodology began with an examination of different regions of the world with regard to ongoing and anticipated change—referred to as "enduring principles," as well as "enduring realities," such as the existence of Russian nuclear weapons. It derived force structure requirements through an assessment of military capabilities of adversaries and regional powers (GAO, 1993). This analysis resulted in the development of force packages for each region—specifying force numbers for each service, the mix of active and reserve forces, and where forces would be located. These force packages were intended to be tools for sizing force requirements, not a blueprint for a new command structure (GAO, 1993). In addition to responding to a new spectrum of conventional threats and regional skirmishes, the review also included analysis of nuclear competition with Russia and implication for forces for strategic deterrence (Snider, 1993).

Establishing a Base Force in the Intelligence Community

Almost two decades after Colin Powell's base force concept was born, it reemerged as a concept for workforce planning in the intelligence community. In 2009, Ron Sanders, CHCO in the ODNI, saw in the base force concept a structured approach to managing a reduction in the size of the intelligence workforce—in response to anticipated budget cuts and evolving strategic challenges. Similar to Powell's post-Vietnam experience, Sanders' review of the drawdown of the intelligence community after the end of the Cold War and before 9/11 made him sensitive to the dangers of downsizing without a plan. The turbulence incurred by rapid drawdown can be a challenge to effectively manage and the long-term consequences difficult to mitigate.

In a 2007 interview, Sanders talked about the consequences of the post–Cold War drawdown: "By design or default, the intelligence community was downsized dramatically in the '90s. Whatever else their faults, our intelligence agencies on 9/11 just didn't have enough people to do the job" (Pourinski, 2007). In 2009, Sanders noted that the intelligence community went through a recent history of "boom and bust" of hiring, firing, and rehiring that has proven disruptive to the intelligence workforce: "[W]e peaked in fiscal '89, '90, and '91, we declined by 40% in the intervening years, we were gutted, and we have been in 'recovery' since we bottomed out in fiscal year 2001" (Cacas, 2009).

Sanders focused on the DNI's concerns that the growth in the community's workforce after 9/11, which helped establish a new level of capability for the intelligence community, might be in jeopardy. He sought to ensure that recent gains in the intelligence workforce were not negated through application of general reductions in personnel resources. The base force became a means of protecting gains from the previous boom-and-bust cycle that proved so hard to manage and from which the community was still recovering.

The base force for the intelligence community was to be derived from the CEP data. In addition to the CEP, community members also submit data on the base force required to execute agency missions in each occupation or job group and compares those requirements with the workforce at hand. Thus the base force would describe the requirements—in number and occupational mix—required to carry out national strategy for the intelligence community. Like Powell's base force, the community's base force would be the minimum workforce requirements to carry out the mission.

Though the catalysts for creating a base force were similar in both DoD and the intelligence community, their analytical approaches diverged significantly. The DoD base force was predicated on planning scenarios that accounted for both regional threats and the projected capabilities of adversaries. By 1990, the development of total force requirements to accomplish specific military missions had significant analytical grounding. In contrast, there were no planning scenarios that could be used to develop requirements for intelligence analysts. The growth in the intelligence workforce and projected requirements for future years emerged less from an explicit link between plans and resources and more from a series of agency-by-agency management initiatives to increase workforce capabilities in light of the deficiencies noted after 9/11. The NIPF provides a valuable structure for articulating and communicating intelligence priorities and could be tied to development of a base force.

In sum, the DoD base force was built from the bottom up using a scenario-based approach; the intelligence community's base force was the result of the end state of individual agencies rebuilding their workforce capability in response to a point at which, in the judgment of intelligence community managers, they could sufficiently meet the threat. To a large extent, the intelligence community's base force is predicated on the notion that, having built up the capability of the community over a decade, with no diminution of the threat, arbitrary budget cuts will leave the agencies of the community in the same precarious positions as they had on the eve of 9/11.

Summary

Effective workforce planning requires understanding of both workforce supply and demand. Only when the two are compared can an organization identify gaps or surpluses in capabilities and determine a strategic approach to bringing the workforce into balance. Because elements of the intelligence community vary in size and organizational affiliation, not every tool described in this and the previous chapter will be applicable to each community element or at any one point in time. What we have described here is a variety of tools that can have utility in intelligence workforce planning and be applied more broadly throughout the community.

CHAPTER SIX

Looking Ahead: Considerations and Guideposts

The intelligence community, along with other national security organizations, faces an era of declining budgets as the rising federal budget deficit puts pressure on departmental resources across the government. But unlike during the period following the end of the Cold War, when budgets fell and threats subsided, the United States continues to face a world filled with highly dynamic security challenges. Global interests and interdependencies have broadened and deepened, creating complexities that require planning agility. And relatively small actors, even individuals, can create economic disruption and significant national security consequences.

In September 2001, the United States found itself unprepared in the face of terrorist attacks on the U.S. homeland. In large measure, the nation was unprepared because of decisions made—or perhaps better stated, the lack of careful planning—as reductions in force structure and personnel were made in the 1990s. The end result ravaged the intelligence community workforce and led to obsolete infrastructure.

Today, the national security community stands at a similar precipice. Budgets are declining. Decisions made in the face of resource constraints will have an impact for decades to come. If the past has taught decisionmakers anything, it is the need to traverse this landscape in a careful and deliberate fashion—not haphazardly, and not without consideration of risk and consequences. During the past decade, the intelligence community has made great strides in rebuilding its workforce and developing a set of workforce planning tools that aid individual agencies in strategic workforce planning and facilitate the ODNI's efforts in community-wide planning as well.

The community must continue to build and sustain its workforce, even as resources decline, making wise and effective decisions on how to prioritize investments—where to strengthen capabilities, where to cut, where to sustain. The lessons learned through an era of workforce rebuilding can inform resource decisions that must be made today, and in the years to come, so that the capabilities attained during the past decade will not be lost. By doing so, the nation will remain prepared to confront the security challenges of the future.

Looking at the community's collective efforts to take a more strategic approach to workforce planning, we identify important considerations that serve as guideposts for the future.

Rebuilding Lost Capability Takes Time

The hiring freeze in the intelligence community during much of the 1990s resulted, by the end of the decade, in a smaller workforce and a loss of the midcareer cadre—a loss from which the community has not yet fully recovered. After a few years of hiring that began soon after 9/11, the resulting workforce was dominated by junior personnel with little experience and very senior personnel with considerable experience but also largely retirement-eligible, or soon to become so. Given that it can take nearly a decade to develop an effective intelligence analyst, losing a cadre of personnel in midcareer with adequate knowledge to mentor junior staff and nearing the point at which they have amassed enough experience to step into leadership positions is a costly outcome.

Declining resources in the years ahead will necessarily lead to workforce adjustments. As the community contemplates this future, it should be mindful of the past decade of rebuilding and why that rebuilding was necessary. The actions taken during the 1990s are particularly poignant in that they occurred during a similar era of budget cuts. But the consequences to the intelligence workforce, however unintended, are consequences that today's leaders should ensure are not repeated. Having a sufficient number of midcareer personnel is essential to building and sustaining an agile and flexible workforce and to developing future leaders. Using the tools described in the previous chapters to forecast future workforce requirements while hedging against risk in a considered and deliberate manner will help workforce planners sustain capabilities and identify needed investments.

Resource Flexibility Is Needed

The intelligence budget offers limited opportunity for flexibility as resources decline. On the one hand, the budget consists of large, very expensive, multiyear capital investment programs—fixed commitments that are incrementally financed. Budgetary disruption, particularly of the degree that would occur should sequestration be enforced, would be considerable and costly. The remainder of the budget relates to personnel. Because of the fixed commitments to capital investment programs, the perceived flexibility in the intelligence budget comes from personnel accounts. But that line of thinking must be approached with caution.

In the intelligence community, as well as DoD, the end-strength reductions that occurred in the 1990s have largely eliminated any margin that could serve as a shock absorber to lessen strategic consequences. Indeed, the community only recently finished implementing the personnel increases recommended by the 9/11 Commission— nearly a decade later. Furthermore, the contractor personnel who are considered core to accomplishing the intelligence mission are embedded in program budgets throughout the intelligence agencies. Thus, how the community structures its personnel accounts is very important in an era of declining budgets.

For both personnel and capital investment accounts, it may be necessary for the executive branch to consider fundamental structural changes to the budget. One such change would be to consolidate individual line items in a manner that would increase flexibility within broader program areas. Using only the personnel accounts to absorb budget cuts would be impossibly risky. But, for those cuts that will undoubtedly be necessary, the full range of workforce planning tools described in the previous chapters will enable the community to identify the best courses of action to balance requirements against available personnel within constrained resources.

Risk Is an Essential Element in Workforce Planning

Future requirements can never be known with certainty because national security priorities and guidance shift over time. Thus, it is prudent to consider risk when evaluating future workforce demands. When threats are of high priority to the national security establishment but also highly volatile, building a hedging strategy into workforce plans can help to mitigate risk. Such an approach can identify areas in which resource commitments need to be sustained, even if near-term conditions might suggest otherwise, as well as conditions under which additional resources might be needed and where they will come from. The volatility methodology developed by RAND researchers helps decisionmakers understand the risks associated with allocating intelligence resources and how to incorporate this understanding as they balance resources across the portfolio of intelligence programs. Being able to more effectively make resource-allocation decisions is particularly valuable when taking into account the lead time needed to acquire certain resources—particularly personnel, who take years to train and develop into effective analysts.

Systematic Planning Shores Up Requirements

Developing workforce requirements by using a systematic process that is based on strategic guidance provides a highly visible means of organizing information about the workforce and its capabilities. One of the distinct benefits of deliberate workforce planning is that it presents an objective framework for communicating requirements to decisionmakers and stakeholders. Workforce requirements are explicitly linked to priorities, and, if those priorities change, it is possible to proactively address changes that may be needed in workforce capabilities. It also illuminates the effect of resource reductions or trade-offs that is particularly valuable in support of difficult decisions undoubtedly required when budgets decline.

The workforce demand forecasting tools, described in this report, are based on a planning hierarchy that begins with the National Security Strategy and the intelligence priorities derived from that strategy. This type of planning foundation provides decisionmakers with sound justification for future workforce requirements and a basis for balancing those requirements against available resources.

Supply of Military Personnel Is Likely to Decline

Military personnel are an important component of the intelligence workforce. They are highly skilled personnel who bring capabilities essential to the community's mission. In recent years, many military personnel positions in the intelligence workforce have been unfilled because of the priority placed on filling requirements associated with the conflicts in Iraq and Afghanistan. And it is likely that these shortfalls will continue with planned force reductions in the Army and Marine Corps—the consequences of which could be that fewer military personnel are assigned to intelligence positions. Today, the community lacks a trained cadre of personnel to fill the gaps created when military positions go unfilled, and it will need to directly confront the task of how to mitigate future shortfalls should they arise, so as not to affect mission effectiveness. Collaboration with the military departments in determining the likely supply of military personnel will be an important part of the process, as will ensuring that positions identified for military personnel truly require the unique attributes they bring to the intelligence mission. That said, the career paths of personnel in the military intelligence career field have not been as robust as those in nonintelligence fields, as evidenced in part by lower retention. This too is something the intelligence and military departments will need to address moving into the future.

In Conclusion

The United States faces complex and evolving national security challenges. Threats exist around the globe from state and nonstate actors alike. The most-significant challenges in the coming decades will include counterterrorism, counterproliferation, cybersecurity, and counterintelligence. But there will be others as well. The U.S. intelligence community has a continuing and important role to play in providing the best intelligence and analytic insight possible to aid the nation's leaders in making decisions and taking action. And executing this role will require unprecedented collaboration and information sharing. The personnel throughout the intelligence agencies—civilian, military, and contractor—are essential to accomplishing these tasks.

The intelligence community has made significant progress during the past decade in rebuilding its workforce and developing capabilities lost during the 1990s. As decisionmakers look ahead to a future most certainly defined by constrained budgets, it will be important to avoid repeating the post–Cold War drawdown experience and losing capability in a similar way because the consequences of such actions can be long lasting. Instead, a proactive approach is called for. As the community navigates this future, the ODNI and community elements should continue to use the workforce planning tools described in this report in order to maintain a workforce capable of meeting the challenges that lie ahead.

An Analysis of Department of Defense Military Intelligence Personnel

Introduction

On December 17, 2004, when President George W. Bush signed into law the IRTPA, he said, "The Director will lead a unified intelligence community. [He or she] will have the authority . . . to establish common standards for the intelligence community's personnel" (White House, 2004). On June 22, 2006, the DNI issued the *Strategic Human Capital Plan: An Annex to the US National Intelligence Strategy* (ODNI, 2006). The human capital plan charged the intelligence community to

> Build an agile, "all source" workforce by projecting and planning for mission critical human resource requirements (both quantitative and qualitative); determining the optimum mix of military, civilian, contractor, and other human resources necessary to meet those requirements; and creating an overarching IC-wide human resource policy. . . . (ODNI, 2006, p. 1)

The plan also suggested that "[b]etter planning and utilization of military members . . . including comprehensive career management, will improve the return on our investment in their hiring and training. This will require close collaboration with the military services" (ODNI, 2006, p. 11). This appendix provides an analysis of the status of military intelligence personnel at the end of FY 2007.[1]

Human Resources of the Intelligence Community

The total workforce of the intelligence community at the end of FY 2007 was composed of four categories of personnel:

- government civilians, 27 percent
- active-duty military of the four military services, 54 percent
- contractors (see ODNI, 2008), 18 percent

---

[1] The analysis, conducted for ODNI in the fall of 2008, reflects the state of military personnel at the end of FY 2007.

- reserve military (approximately 15,000 Selected Reserves that actively drill and approximately 8,000 in the Individual Ready Reserve who can be called up in an emergency).

Each component brings a unique set of capabilities and strengths that represent a limited and valuable resource. Ideally, the individual components should be developed and managed to ensure that they complement each other. Ideally, balance should be attained across the components so that the unique capabilities of each component can be leveraged to enhance overall effectiveness. In this context, active-duty military intelligence personnel should be viewed as a unique asset that provide capabilities that complement but are distinct from other components. Doing this effectively requires that both the intelligence community and the military services recognize and provide for the needs of each other. This military annex focuses on the active-duty military that serve in the intelligence career fields.

Military of the Intelligence Community

Military personnel make up the largest single source of human capital that staff positions throughout the intelligence community. The DNI is responsible for directing and overseeing the NIP, in which a significant number of military personnel are employed. The NIP includes the CIA Program, National Reconnaissance Program, Consolidated Cryptologic Program, General Defense Intelligence Program, and the National Geospatial-Intelligence Program.

Most military personnel are employed in the MIP and are used to acquire intelligence for the planning and conduct of tactical military operations. The MIP is directed and controlled by the Secretary of Defense. Portions of the budgets of the military departments, defense agencies, and U.S. Special Operations Command and its components finance the MIP. The MIP program executive is the Under Secretary of Defense for Intelligence. In general, the MIP has more junior and company-grade officers and enlisted personnel than the NIP, which has more senior personnel.

Military personnel with intelligence occupational specialty codes are managed as a total group without regard to the position or billets they currently hold, be they positions in the NIP or MIP. Over the course of their careers, military personnel can expect to serve in both NIP and MIP positions. Regardless of their current positions, military intelligence personnel are managed under a set of general regulations that describe how prospective enlisted members and officers are recruited, trained, promoted, retained, and eventually retired. This "life cycle" is not specific to military personnel with intelligence skills but is prescribed for all military personnel in general. The Defense Officer Personnel Management Act of 1980 (DOPMA) (Pub. L. 96-513) prescribes the system for officers. The system for enlisted personnel is set by a series of personnel policies with grade limitations placed on DoD by Congress. For example, Congress sets the proportion of the enlisted force that can hold the top four enlisted ranks.

Managing Military Personnel Under the Defense Officer Personnel Management Act

The typical officer personnel profile is built into the various provisions of DOPMA and is reflected in the associated pay tables. It is the combination of policy restrictions and pay that experience has shown is most important to service members when they decide whether they will remain in the force after their initial service obligations are completed or leave active-duty military service. A substantial body of research has shown empirically how military personnel consider the timing and likelihood of promotions, the year-of-service limits on their careers, and the size and timing of their compensation packages in their decisions. The provisions of DOPMA are key to the decisions made by officers (see Rostker, 2006).

Structurally, DOPMA provides a set of grade tables that tie the military end strength of the service to a distribution of military grades of O-1 (second lieutenant) to O-6 (colonel) (Rostker et al., 1993). DOPMA determines the year of service in which an officer can be promoted from one grade to the next and the proportion of eligible officers that may be promoted. It also provides the high tenure rules for separation and mandatory retirement.[2]

The personnel profile of the U.S. military officer is unique among major military powers. In Europe, for example, career officers routinely serve until their late fifties.[3] In the United States, only the highest-ranking flag and general officers serve past their early fifties. DOPMA allows full retirement as early as 20 years of service, with mandatory retirement of all officers who have not reached the grade of O-7 by 30 years of service. As a result, the U.S. military retires large numbers of highly skilled and proficient career officers who, by most accounts, still could provide years of productive service.

The Guiding Principles for the Management of Military Personnel

Since the end of World War II, there has been a continuing debate about the guiding principles for the management of military personnel. The debate can be summed up in two competing ideas: "youth and vigor" versus "experience and performance." Although the current system favors the former with a competitive "up-or-out" system for all grades, voluntary retirement at 20 years of service and mandatory retirement for those not promoted to flag or general officer grades by 30 years of service,[4] the issue

---

[2] The move to create a DOPMA-like system for enlisted personnel is discussed in Rostker, 2006.

[3] For example, Thie et al., 1994, note,

> Generally foreign military career officers, especially those in the field-grade ranks, are expected to remain in service until established retirement points. The earliest career mandatory retirement point noted was at age 55, and this was often for officers in the grades of major or below. In many cases, there were provisions for extended service up to age 60 for career officers in ranks higher than major. (p. 116)

[4] Those who fail to promote to the highest enlisted grades or to the grade of colonel are mandatorily retired before 30 years of service.

resonates for the future of military intelligence officers in which "experience and performance" are paramount.

During the congressional debate on DOPMA, Senator Sam Nunn expressed concern that the new act would "rigidify the already too rigid up or out system." It would

> prohibit the continuation on active duty of . . . highly qualified officers even when they wish to continue and the Services need them . . . requiring the separation of all officers below the grade of O-4 [major] who are not selected for promotion to the next higher grade. (Nunn, 1976)

The Assistant Secretary of Defense for Manpower, Reserve Affairs and Logistics, countered, arguing that keeping officers who have been passed over would not

> assist us in keeping skilled people, and the motivation, effectiveness, and productivity of those who stay are seriously questionable. The Services' past experiences with extended grade stagnations do not support the long term utility of a system that demands more of people who have been identified as having limited potential. . . . The positive incentive of promotion is preferable to one that continues others in a second class category. (White, 1977)

The Defense Manpower Commission established by Congress in 1974 saw that the more pressing issue was forcing senior officers to leave because of the low selection rates in the senior grades of O-5 and O-6. It argued that "it is inconceivable that a Service member who has been screened many times during his Service life . . . is suddenly of no further value to his Service simply because the Service does not have enough promotions to go around" (Defense Manpower Commission, 1976, p. 261).[5]

In 1992, the Senate Armed Services Committee directed that DoD reconsider DOPMA, arguing that a post-drawdown

> smaller officer corps—smallest in size since 1950—should be managed under rules that provide for less turnover and greater stability. Longer careers should be the rule rather than the exception and up-or-out features of DOPMA should be adjusted accordingly. . . . At the same time, the committee recognizes the need for stable

---

5 The commission recommended,

> Careful selection into the career force should replace management out of the career force that is embodied in an "up-or-out" system. Recognizing that there may be situations requiring reduction in the career force that exceed its normal elasticity, selection-out authority should be granted to the Service Secretary. . . . A procedure for screening career force members for effective performance should be developed by each Service. This procedure should be unassociated with selection for promotion and should occur periodically. Any persons determined not to be performing effectively should be separated from the Service and receive separation payments. . . . A promotion system based on years-of-service ranges of eligibility is preferable to a phase point concept. Time in grade as well as being in the range should be a condition of promotion eligibility. (Defense Manpower Commission, 1976, pp. 261–262)

career advancement patterns in each Military Service that encourages longer careers. (cited in Thie et al., 1994, pp. 199–200)

Analysis done to meet the 1992 study mandate found that the argument about maximum career lengths pivots on the requirement for youth and vigor but concluded that "there is no analytical evidence for maximum career lengths as they exist now or for any particular career length applied as a group standard to officers in all skills" (Thie et al., 1994, p. 99). These findings not withstanding, DOPMA was not changed and continues to dictate how officers, including intelligence officers, are managed. Enlisted personnel are managed in an analogous manner.

Managing Officers by Competitive Category

The DOPMA system is not strictly a "one-size-fits-all" system. DOPMA provides that officers can compete against similar officers if they are placed in the same "competitive category." The Secretary of Defense charges the secretaries of the military departments to

> establish competitive categories, as required, to manage, in relation to the requirements of the officer category concerned, the career development and promotion of certain groups of officers whose specialized education, training, or experience, and often relatively narrow utilization, make separate career management desirable. (Under Secretary of Defense for Personnel and Readiness, 2005, p. 3)

The Secretary of the Navy establishes policy for the Navy and Marine Corps. The Department of the Navy policy is

> to establish officer competitive categories to provide for separate promotion consideration and career development of groups of officers with related education, training, skills, and experience needed to meet mission objectives of the Navy or Marine Corps which make separate career management desirable. (Secretary of the Navy, 2006, p. 1)

In the Navy, intelligence officers are in a separate competitive category. In the Marine Corps (and in the Air Force), they are part of the unrestricted officer competitive category and compete with other, nonintelligence officers for promotion.

There are six competitive categories in the Army for company-grade officers. All branches and functional areas other than the special branches are in a single competitive category. Chaplain and staff judge advocate are in separate categories. The Army Medical Department has a category for the Medical and Dental Corps and a category for all other Medical Department branches (see Department of the Army, 2007). Under the Officer Personnel Management System (OPMS) XXI, all officers other than those assigned to the special branches with the rank of major and higher are separated into one of three functional categories: operations, operations support, and information operations and institutional support. Although they compete against other officers in the same functional categories, the precepts to the promotion boards generally ensure an equitable distribution of promotions.

Management by competitive category does provide the potential to group intelligence officers together for both promotion and career development and to alter the basic provision of DOPMA to fit the needs of the competitive category. Today, for example, the medical and dental competitive categories are not subject to the grade table restriction of DOPMA. However, they continue to be subject to the DOPMA high tenure rules.

Military Manpower and Personnel: Managing Faces and Spaces

Although it is the policy of DoD "to provide an adequate officer inventory to meet projected manpower and skill requirements for each competitive category and grade, that . . . should reflect the appropriate distribution of officers by grade, experience, and skill" (Under Secretary of Defense for Personnel and Readiness, 2005, p. 2), the overall number of military personnel that Congress authorizes is only loosely related to the total billets the military services recognize. The congressional authorization is a "top-down" number based on political considerations. Although, in the recent past, the Quadrennial Defense Review has recommended to Congress changes in military end strength, the end strength of the services has been relatively stable since the drawdown after the end of the Cold War, even when considering the increases related to the global war on terrorism. The mismatch between authorizations and positions is managed by priority. High-priority positions or billets are routinely filled, with lower-priority billets regularly "gapped" for some period of time or just left vacant.

One reason that changes have been small is the dynamics of military personnel management. The military personnel system is an "in-at-the-bottom, up-through-the-ranks" system. In practice, the system has only one entry point, at zero years of service. Lateral entry from the civilian labor force is rarely allowed. In other words, efforts to grow a larger force are generally limited by the military's ability to attract new accessions and absorb new personnel, giving them the required training and experiences to grow their capabilities, which is particularly significant for the intelligence community. A larger force can also come about if there is an improvement in the retention of personnel already in service.

Managing the Military Personnel Community

Military Intelligence Occupation Strength Trends

Military personnel with intelligence specialties are a relatively small proportion of the total number of people serving in the military. Table A.1 shows the proportion of intelligence personnel for each of the military services in FY 2007, ranging from 7 percent for the Air Force to less than 2 percent for the Marine Corps.

In the past several years, the number of military personnel carrying intelligence military occupation designators has remained essentially constant, as shown in Table A.2. During this period, the end strengths of the Army and the Marine Corps grew 6.43 percent and 3.66 percent, respectively. Their intelligence end strengths grew at greater rates, 9.5 percent and 13.1 percent, respectively. The Navy and Air Force overall military end strengths decreased by –7.15 percent and –5.80 percent, respectively. The intelligence end strengths decreased in the Navy by –24.6 percent, with the Air Force remaining essentially unchanged (an increase of 0.03 percent). The change was less than proportional for the Air Force but greater than proportional for the Navy.

Meeting Intelligence Personnel Requirements

The current inventory of intelligence personnel is insufficient to fill all the positions that the services (in the MIP) and ODNI (in the NIP) recognize as valid requirements. The individual components of the intelligence community have told the DNI that

Table A.1
Intelligence Personnel as a Percentage of the Military Force, Fiscal Year 2007

Service	Nonintelligence	Intelligence	
		Number	Percentage
Army	491,047	26,736	5.16
Navy	321,843	10,426	3.14
Air Force	305,250	23,844	7.25
Marine Corps	182,911	3,514	1.88

SOURCE: Defense Manpower Data Center.

Table A.2
Intelligence Personnel, by Service and Fiscal Year

Service	FY 2005	FY 2006	FY 2007	Change 2005–2007 (%)
Army	24,406	25,333	26,736	9.55
Navy	13,834	11,667	10,426	−24.63
Air Force	23,838	24,558	23,844	0.03
Marine Corps	3,106	3,179	3,514	13.14
Total	65,184	64,737	64,520	−1.02

SOURCE: Defense Manpower Data Center.

they have budgeted for more military positions than the services are able to fill. The Secretary of Defense has provided the services guidance to fill the operational billets in Iraq and Afghanistan first before filling the NIP positions based in the continental United States.

The Accession and Retention of Intelligence Personnel

The number of military intelligence specialists in the services at any point in time is based on previous yearly accessions, the number of personnel cross-trained and assigned during their careers, and the voluntary retention of personnel. By far, the retention of personnel is the most important. Pushing more candidates in at the bottom, with associated recruitment and training costs, will have only a minimum impact if they do not decide to stay after their initial service obligations are completed. Moving personnel into the intelligence career fields in the middle of their careers can accommodate excess in other career fields, but it takes time to train and provide them with the range of experiences expected of midcareer intelligence personnel. The most cost-effective program, and one anticipated in the *Human Capital Plan* (ODNI, 2006), e.g., "improve the return on our investment in their hiring and training," is to improve retention. However, improving retention may be problematic given the current situation.

Analysis of Air Force Intelligence Personnel

Using the Air Force as an example, we can see the current personnel situation by examining the year-to-year continuation rates and the resulting year-of-service personnel profile for Air Force enlisted personnel and officers.[6] Figure A.1 shows the continuation rates for Air Force enlisted personnel who have an Air Force specialty code (AFSC, analogous to an Army military occupational specialty [MOS], the term we use throughout the rest of this appendix) for intelligence specialists. The pattern is typical of continuation rates for today's all-volunteer force. The initial drop shows early attrition from basic training and initial skill training. Retention rises and is high over the next several years as military personnel complete their initial military service obligation. Depending on the program they join, this obligation may be for four, five, or six years.

The drop in retention at the fourth and sixth years of service in Figure A.1 reflects members who complete their obligated service and decide to return to civilian life. Continuation rates rise after that point because members who decide to stay are more interested in making the military a career. The draw of the retirement system, with the opportunity to retire after 20 years of service, is reflected in the very high continuation rates after ten years of service. There is a sharp drop in continuation at the 20-year point as personnel exercise their option to retire. Continuation patterns after 25 years

---

[6]   A note at the end of this appendix discusses the data used in this analysis.

Figure A.1
Air Force Enlisted Intelligence Continuation Rates, by Years of Service

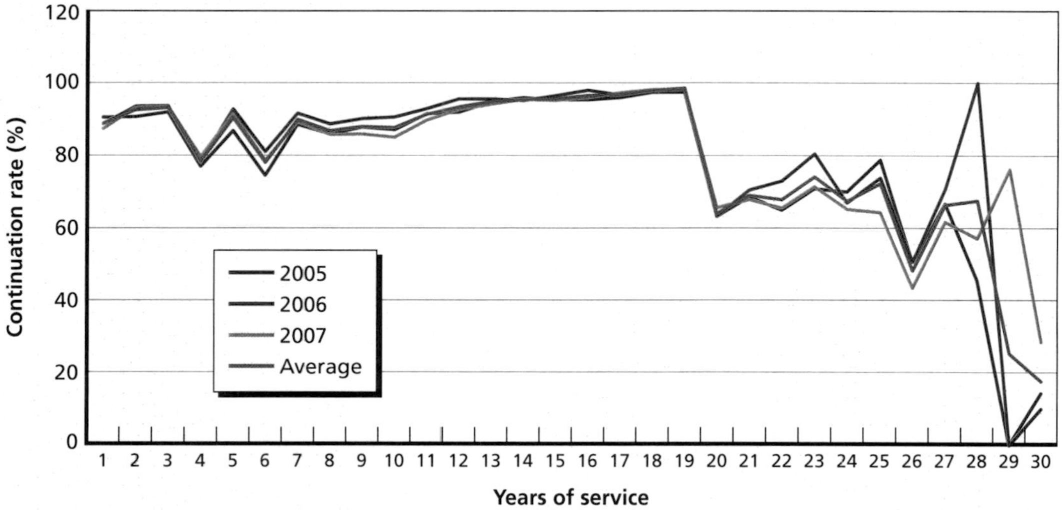

SOURCE: Authors' analysis of Defense Manpower Data Center data.
RAND *RR114-A.1*

of service are very volatile because there are very few service members with intelligence specialties in these year groups.

A comparison of the continuation rates for intelligence and nonintelligence cadres provides some indication of how the Air Force's enlisted intelligence specialists are doing compared with all other occupations, as shown in Figure A.2. The yellow line shows the deviation in the continuation rate between intelligence and nonintelligence occupations by year of service. The effect of this deviation is shown in Figure A.3, which is the normalized year-of-service profile.

The areas under the curves are the expected man-years of service from each cohort of 100 recruits. The higher the curve, e.g., the more the curve lies to the upper right of the chart, the more years of service each cohort will produce and the higher will be the return on the investment made in their hiring and training. Figure A.3 shows the year-of-service profile for the intelligence and nonintelligence Air Force enlisted occupations. The two profiles are almost identical, suggesting that the intelligence occupations are performing about the same as the nonintelligence occupations. Unfortunately, this is not always the case for all Air Force personnel.

The continuation rate pattern for Air Force officers, Figure A.4, shows substantial deviation from the pattern for nonintelligence officers. The resulting year-of-service profile comparison (Figure A.5) shows that Air Force intelligence officers are leaving much earlier than their nonintelligence colleagues, and an initial cohort produces fewer man-years of service. Given that the NIP generally employs officers in the grade of O-4 and above, the Air Force is currently producing 88 percent fewer field-grade

Figure A.2
Average Air Force Intelligence and Nonintelligence Enlisted Continuation Rates, by Years of Service, Fiscal Years 2005 to 2007

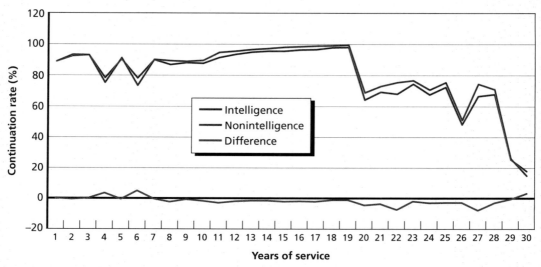

SOURCE: Authors' analysis of Defense Manpower Data Center data.
RAND *RR114-A.2*

Figure A.3
Normalized Air Force Enlisted Personnel Profile, Fiscal Years 2005 to 2007

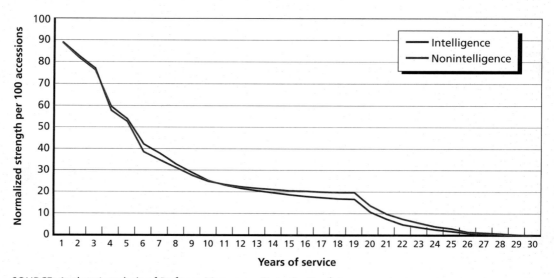

SOURCE: Authors' analysis of Defense Manpower Data Center data.
RAND *RR114-A.3*

Figure A.4
Average Air Force Intelligence and Nonintelligence Officer Continuation Rates, by Years of Service, Fiscal Years 2005 to 2007

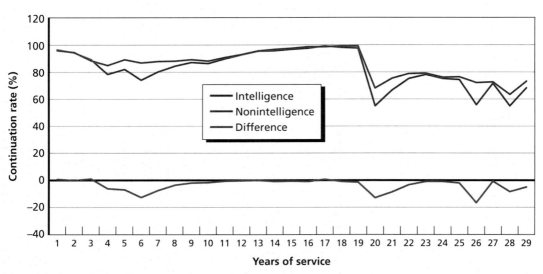

SOURCE: Authors' analysis of Defense Manpower Data Center data.
RAND *RR114-A.4*

Figure A.5
Normalized Air Force Officer Personnel Profile, Fiscal Years 2005 to 2007

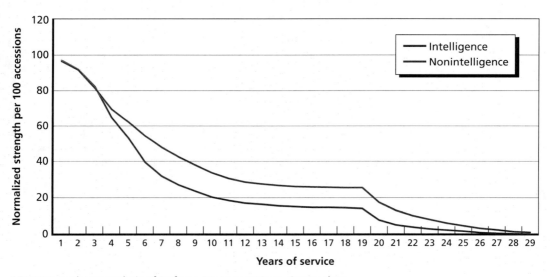

SOURCE: Authors' analysis of Defense Manpower Data Center data.
RAND *RR114-A.5*

officers—major to colonel—than it would if intelligence occupations had the profile exhibited by the nonintelligence occupations.

One possible reason that so many Air Force intelligence officers are leaving is that they are more likely than nonintelligence officers to be employed by contractors or to become employees of the federal government after they leave the Air Force. The DNI noted in the *Human Capital Plan*,

> Increasingly, the IC finds itself in competition with its contractors for [its] own employees. Confronted by arbitrary staffing ceilings and uncertain funding, components are left with no choice but to use contractors for work that may be borderline "inherently governmental"—only to find that to do that work, those same contractors recruit our own employees, already cleared and trained at government expense, and then "lease" them back to us at considerably greater expense. (ODNI, 2006, p. 6)

Figure A.6 shows the postservice employment pattern for Air Force officers who leave before retirement (separatees) and those who retire (retirees) based on their continuing to hold a security clearance. The large number of separatees who are in the guard or reserve retain their clearances because they still have to complete their reserve military service obligation. Contractors and government employees who are also in the guard or reserve are counted as contractors or government employees, respectively.

Figure A.6
Status of Air Force Officer Separatees and Retirees After Leaving Active Service, Fiscal Years 2004 to 2006

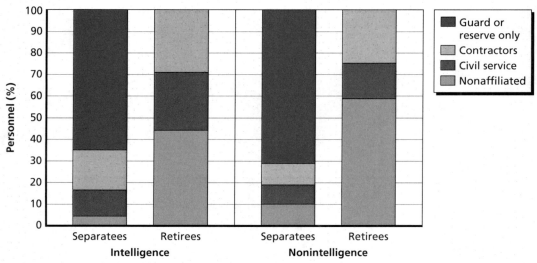

SOURCE: Authors' analysis of Defense Manpower Data Center data.
RAND RR114-A.6

Figure A.7
Average Air Force Intelligence Officer Gains and Losses, Fiscal Years 2005 to 2007

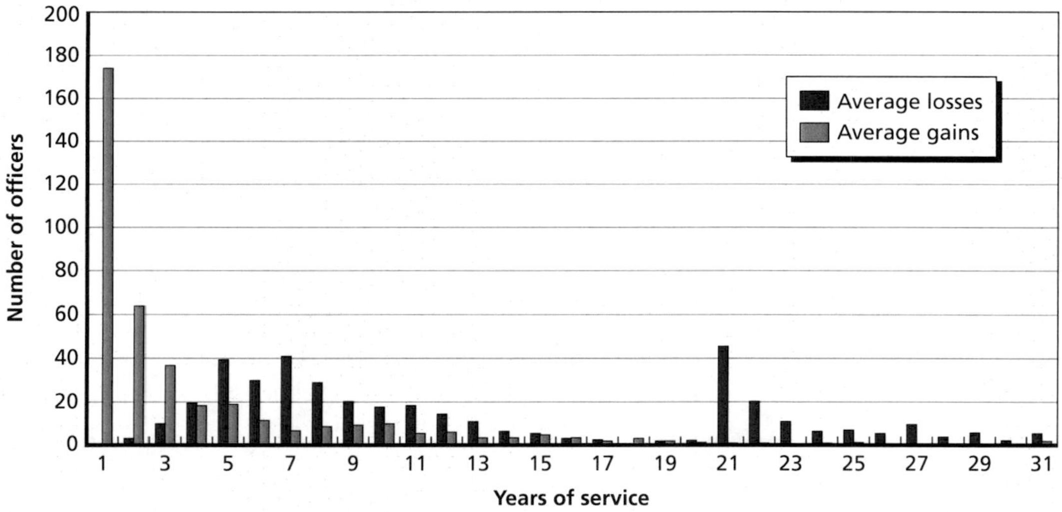

SOURCE: Authors' analysis of Defense Manpower Data Center data.
RAND RR114-A.7

Another potential source of intelligence officers is from lateral transfer from other military occupations during a career. An analysis of the gains and losses of Air Force intelligence officers between FY 2005 and FY 2007 (Figure A.7) shows that the vast majority of new intelligence officers were gained during their first term of service and relatively few were transferred later in their careers.

Personnel Profiles for the Other Services

The personnel profiles for the other services are more like the problematic profile for Air Force officers than they are like the profile exhibited by Air Force enlisted intelligence personnel. Figure A.8 shows the personnel profile for the services for enlisted personnel with intelligence MOS codes; Figure A.9 shows the personnel profiles for intelligence officers. Although the Marine Corps enlisted profile looks like the Air Force enlisted profile, the profile for the other services is not as robust. The Army and Navy continuation rates show that they produce fewer years of service per accession, with fewer new recruits making it to the senior grades.

Officer year-of-service profiles for the other services look remarkably similar to the Air Force officer profile. However, when the Army and Marine Corps intelligence officer profiles are compared with the profiles for their respective nonintelligence officer groups, they are dramatically less robust. The Marine Corps can expect to get 114 percent fewer field-grade officers from an entering cohort of new intelligence officers than do other Marine Corps officer programs. The Army can expect to get 88 percent fewer field-grade officers from an entering cohort of new intelligence officers than

Figure A.8
Enlisted Intelligence Occupations, Normalized Personnel Profile, by Service

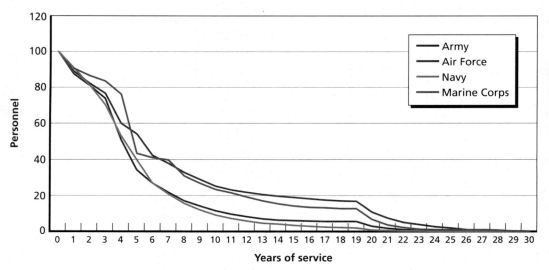

SOURCE: Authors' analysis of Defense Manpower Data Center data.
RAND *RR114-A.8*

Figure A.9
Officer Intelligence Occupations, Normalized Personnel Profiles, by Service

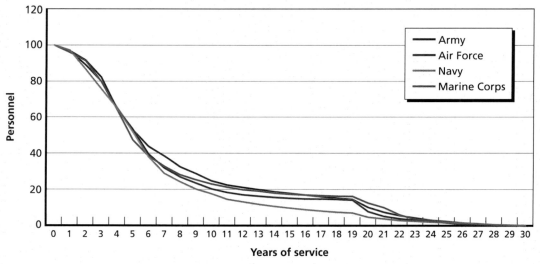

SOURCE: Authors' analysis of Defense Manpower Data Center data.
RAND *RR114-A.9*

do other Army officer programs. This means that the Army's Strategic Intelligence Functional Area, which is made up of only field-grade officers, will have fewer candidates to choose from than other Army officer programs.

Policy Changes to Improve the Utilization of Intelligence Officers and Enlisted Personnel

The requirements for intelligence professionals, particularly the intelligence officers who serve in the NIP, are well articulated by the Army in its description of the "unique functions" performed by the Strategic Intelligence Functional Area officers. Specifically, the Army notes,

> Strategic Intelligence functional area provides a focused, trained corps of strategic intelligence professionals to Army organizations, combatant commands, DOD, the Joint Staff, and interagency communities with tailored intelligence required for the development of national security policy and theater strategic plans and operations. The Strategic Intelligence officer acts as the premier expert on strategic and global intelligence activities that accomplish U.S. strategic objectives developed through unique training, education, and recurring assignments at theater, national, Joint, DOD, and interagency communities. The Strategic Intelligence officer translates national security strategy into intelligence strategies. Providing premier intelligence in a strategic context, the Strategic Intelligence officer enables decisionmakers and warfighters to dominate the battlespace. The Strategic Intelligence officer represents Army interests at the Joint and interagency communities.
>
> Strategic Intelligence officers work primarily at echelons above corps worldwide. [They fill positions] in intelligence units, headquarters, national agencies and unified commands. Strategic Intelligence officers . . . participate in all phases of the intelligence cycle. The Strategic Intelligence officer is an agile, national and theater level and interagency expert—who leads, plans and directs all-source analysis, intelligence systems, and intelligence policy and programs—supporting key decisionmakers, policymakers and warfighters in an interagency, joint, coalition, and combined environment. Exercising broad responsibility and authority, the Strategic Intelligence officer is capable of integrating interagency activities and interacting with the foreign intelligence services to produce predictive strategic intelligence to advise policymakers and combatant commanders to deliver overwhelming advantage to our warfighters, defense planners, and national security policymakers. (Department of the Army, 2007, p. 251)

The personnel system of the military today is ill suited to produce the kind and number of officers needed by the intelligence community. Today's system is built on the paradigm of youth and vigor. It is designed to produce a relatively small number of personnel with the kind of training and experiences that are required of today's intelligence professionals. The grade table that drives the system reflects the needs of combat units, not the needs of the interagency intelligence community. The DOPMA high tenure and retirement rules truncate and terminate military careers just when intelligence officers have gained the experiences necessary to make them truly productive. The best that can be said is that many former intelligence personnel continue to serve as government employees and contractors.

The "up or out" culture and associated policies of the services force personnel who are not selected for promotion to senior grades to retire at a relatively young age at the end of a 20-year career. Although this is acceptable, even advantageous, for many of the combat arms, it is counterproductive for intelligence professionals. Changing this system will require the services to retain personnel with demonstrated professional intelligence expertise and experience beyond current mandatory retirement dates and may also require statutory relief to allow them to do so. Thus, relief from both grade and tenure restrictions is necessary.

It is clear from the personnel profiles presented here that intelligence officers and enlisted specialists perceive the disadvantages of their career fields and the opportunities that their training and experience provides them, and many more choose to leave military service than do similar officers from other military occupations. The twin (and related) problems of having a dysfunctional career profile and poor retention mean that there will be fewer military intelligence personnel who will gain the experience needed and will be available to serve the intelligence community. One way to address this problem is to build a career profile based on the paradigm of "experience and performance."

Note: Career Profile and Postservice Employment Data and Analysis

The Year-of-Service Profile of Officers and Enlisted Personnel of the Intelligence Community

The use of numerical models for manpower analysis and management using longitudinal personnel record is a well-established practice. Personnel planning, as we know it today, can be traced to at least 1679 in Great Britain, when the Secretary of the Admiralty started to regulate the annual entry of officers into the Royal Navy. By 1779, the Royal Marines were managing career structures, retention rates, and promotion probabilities. Commander Roy C. Smith presented the simple mathematics of personnel planning in his paper "Personnel and Promotion Reduced to Its Simplest Terms" in 1906 (Smith, 1906). The challenge to modern personnel-planning systems is not the lack of conceptual planning models. It is the commitment to collect and manage the mass of data required to "feed" these models and, as in the case of the intelligence community, making sure that "the right questions are asked." The data necessary to model the military personnel systems, both officers and enlisted personnel, are systematically collected by the Defense Manpower Data Center. The particular challenge in modeling the intelligence community is understanding the intraservice flow into and out of the community.

Simple comparisons of end-strength numbers between years of service provide misleading and useless numbers. A careful and full accounting of the flows of personnel into and out of categories is required, as illustrated in Figure A.10. As a rule, a continuation rate cannot be greater than one; in other words, the number of people who complete one year cannot be greater than the number of those who start the following year, and yet we see, by simply comparing year-end numbers with year-beginning numbers, that the (gross) continuations rates are often well over one. That is because the gross continuation rate uses data that contained interservice transfers into and out of the intelligence community, rather than only data on those who leave the service. When these interservice transfers are fully accounted for and removed, as they are in the net continuation rates shown in Figure A.10, the expected pattern of continuation rates is apparent.

Table A.3 shows the final categories used to fully account for the interservice flows into and out of the intelligence community. The table shows the flows for officers, warrant officers, and enlisted personnel. Separate tables were developed for three fiscal years from 2005 to 2008, and the average of the three years was computed as the representative rate for each year-of-service cell. These average rates for each year-of-service cell are shown in Figure A.10 and used to construct the various figures in this

Figure A.10
Comparison of Gross and Net Continuation Rates, by Year of Service, for Military Officers of the Army Intelligence Community

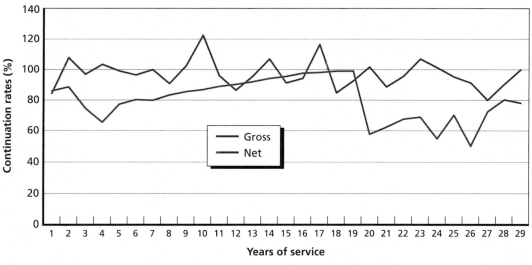

SOURCE: Authors' analysis of Defense Manpower Data Center data.
RAND RR114-A.10

Table A.3
Categorization of Interservice Transfers of the Active-Duty Army Intelligence Community, Fiscal Year 2005

Population	Category
Enlisted	**Beginning FY strength**

	FY losses to enlisted intelligence
	Left enlisted intelligence population and transferred to warrant intelligence
	Left enlisted intelligence population and transferred to commissioned
	    intelligence
	Left intelligence and the Army
	Left intelligence but remained in the Army
	    Total FY losses to enlisted intelligence

	Remained in enlisted intelligence[a]
	FY gains to enlisted intelligence Transferred from warrant intelligence population Transferred from commissioned intelligence population New to intelligence and the Army New to intelligence but was in the Army in prior FY Total FY gains to enlisted intelligence
	End FY strength Net FY gain (+) or loss (–) to enlisted intelligence
Warrant officer	**Beginning FY strength**

	FY losses to warrant intelligence
	Left warrant intelligence population and transferred to enlisted intelligence
	Left warrant intelligence population and transferred to commissioned
	    intelligence
	Left intelligence and the Army
	Left intelligence but remained in the Army
	    Total FY losses to warrant intelligence

	Remained in warrant intelligence
	FY gains to warrant intelligence Transferred from enlisted intelligence population Transferred from commissioned intelligence population New to intelligence and the Army New to intelligence but was in the Army in the prior FY Total FY gains to warrant intelligence
	End FY strength Net FY gain (+) or loss (–) to warrant intelligence

Table A.3—Continued

Population	Category
Commissioned officer	**Beginning FY strength**
	FY losses to commissioned intelligence
	Left commissioned intelligence population and transferred to enlisted intelligence
	Left commissioned intelligence population and transferred to warrant intelligence
	Left intelligence and the Army
	Left intelligence but remained in the Army
	Total FY losses to commissioned intelligence
	Remained in commissioned intelligence[a]
	FY gains to commissioned intelligence
	Transferred from enlisted intelligence population
	Transferred from warrant intelligence population
	New to intelligence and the Army
	New to intelligence but was in the Army in the prior FY
	Total FY gains to commissioned intelligence
	End FY strength
	Net FY gain (+) or loss (–) to commissioned intelligence
Total	**Beginning FY strength**
	FY losses to intelligence
	Left intelligence and the Army
	Left intelligence but remained in the Army
	Total FY losses to intelligence
	Remained in intelligence[a]
	Remained in intelligence with no grade category change
	Remained in intelligence and transferred to a new grade category
	Total remained in intelligence
	FY gains to intelligence
	New to intelligence and the Army
	New to intelligence but was in the Army in the prior FY
	Total FY gains to intelligence
	End FY strength
	Net FY gain (+) or loss (–) to intelligence

SOURCES: Active-duty master files 200409, 200509; intelligence occupation definitions provided by RAND/DIA; list produced by the Defense Manpower Data Center on April 1, 2008.

[a] Completed years of service: For members who left the Army, years of service is the prior-year years of service plus one year.

appendix. The data were tabulated by the Defense Manpower Data Center based on data provided to it by the individual military services.

Postservice Employment

When we look at the totality of the human resources who work in the intelligence community, a critical question is what happens to intelligence personnel when they leave active duty? Are they lost to the community, or do they continue to contribute in a different status? More specifically, do those who separate before retirement participate

Table A.4
Current Status of the Intelligence Population Who Separated from the U.S. Air Force, Fiscal Years 2004–2006

Current DEERS Status For Separated USAF Intel Populations
By FY, Rank and DEERS Status
DEERS Status As of May 13, 2008, Rank Breakouts From Respective Active Duty Master Edit File

FY2004 Intel Population Who Have Separated From The USAF

	No Current Affiliation	Killed In Action	Reserve/Guard Only	Reserve/Guard and DoD Civilian	Reserve/Guard and Other Civil Service	Reserve/Guard and DoD Contractor	Reserve/Guard and Other Contractor	Retired	Retired and DoD Civilian	Retired and Other Civil Service	Retired and DoD Contractor	Retired and Other Contractor	DoD Civilian	Other Civil Service	DoD Contractor	Other Contractor	Total
			Reserve/Guard Status						Retired Status								
Enlisted	556	0	590	84	0	175	5	454	54	0	73	0	225	0	255	4	2,475
Officer	8	0	133	2	0	5	1	46	20	0	15	0	27	0	47	0	305
Total	564	0	723	86	0	180	6	500	74	0	88	1	252	0	302	4	2,760

FY2005 Intel Population Who Have Separated From The USAF

	No Current Affiliation	Killed In Action	Reserve/Guard Only	Reserve/Guard and DoD Civilian	Reserve/Guard and Other Civil Service	Reserve/Guard and DoD Contractor	Reserve/Guard and Other Contractor	Retired	Retired and DoD Civilian	Retired and Other Civil Service	Retired and DoD Contractor	Retired and Other Contractor	DoD Civilian	Other Civil Service	DoD Contractor	Other Contractor	Total
			Reserve/Guard Status						Retired Status								
Enlisted	498	0	499	44	0	102	6	516	24	0	97	0	181	0	246	2	2,215
Officer	11	0	117	8	0	8	1	45	26	0	22	0	29	0	29	1	289
Total	509	0	616	44	0	110	7	561	50	0	119	0	210	0	275	3	2,504

FY2006 Intel Population Who Have Separated From The USAF

	No Current Affiliation	Killed In Action	Reserve/Guard Only	Reserve/Guard and DoD Civilian	Reserve/Guard and Other Civil Service	Reserve/Guard and DoD Contractor	Reserve/Guard and Other Contractor	Retired	Retired and DoD Civilian	Retired and Other Civil Service	Retired and DoD Contractor	Retired and Other Contractor	DoD Civilian	Other Civil Service	DoD Contractor	Other Contractor	Total
			Reserve/Guard Status						Retired Status								
Enlisted	632	0	608	34	0	124	1	539	39	0	125	0	151	0	260	0	2,513
Officer	14	0	222	1	0	3	2	64	47	0	63	0	29	0	35	2	482
Total	646	0	830	35	0	127	3	603	86	0	188	0	180	0	295	2	2,995

SOURCE: Defense Enrollment Eligibility Reporting System (DEERS).

as military reservists, nonmilitary government civilians, or contractors? Note that both government civilians and contractors may also be members of the reserves after they leave active duty. Similarly, do those who retire from active duty continue to work in the community as government employees or contractors?

Unfortunately, there is no direct way to answer these questions. Separatees and retirees are not systematically surveyed as to their post–active duty employment. There is, however, one thing that they have in common if they are to continue to work in the intelligence community—the need for a security clearance and security identification badges based on the sponsorship of the agency that employs them. This information is contained in the master file of DEERS.

Table A.4 shows the security status of the officer and enlisted intelligence personnel of the U.S. Air Force who left service in FYs 2004, 2005, and 2006, respectively. For example, during FY 2006, a total of 2,995 officers and enlisted personnel left service, with all but 646 maintaining their security clearances. A great many, some 830, continued their association with the intelligence community through their affiliation with the Air National Guard or the Air Force Reserve. In addition, many more were both affiliated with a reserve component and working as civilian employees of the government or a contractor. About one-third of those who retired continued their affiliation with the community as either DoD civilian employees or contractors. Finally, about one-third of the other separatees, those not affiliated with a reserve component, became civilian employees of DoD or worked for a DoD contractor.

Bibliography

9/11 Commission—*See* National Commission on Terrorist Attacks Upon the United States.

Ballenstedt, Brittany, "Two Federal Programs Snare Top Public Service Awards," *Government Executive*, September 10, 2008. As of March 1, 2013:
http://www.govexec.com/defense/2008/09/
two-federal-programs-snare-top-public-service-awards/27628/

Best, Richard A., Jr., *Intelligence Reform After Five Years: The Role of the Director of National Intelligence*, Washington, D.C.: Congressional Research Service, R41295, June 22, 2010. As of March 1, 2013:
http://www.fas.org/sgp/crs/intel/R41295.pdf

Blair, Dennis C., prepared statement for the U.S. Senate Committee on Homeland Security and Governmental Affairs hearing titled "Ten Years After 9/11: Is Intelligence Reform Working? Part II," May 19, 2011. As of March 1, 2013:
http://www.hsgac.senate.gov/download/2011-05-19-blair-testimony

Bush, George W., *Commission on the Intelligence Capabilities of the United States Regarding Weapons of Mass Destruction*, Washington, D.C.: White House, Executive Order 13328, February 6, 2004. As of April 19, 2013:
http://2001-2009.state.gov/t/isn/rls/other/29155.htm

———, *Further Amendments to Executive Order 12333, United States Intelligence Activities*, Washington, D.C.: White House, Executive Order 13470, July 30, 2008. As of April 19, 2013:
http://www.fas.org/irp/offdocs/eo/eo-13470.htm

Cacas, Max, "Intelligence Community Plans Workforce of the Future," *Federal News Radio*, November 24, 2009. As of March 1, 2013:
http://www.federalnewsradio.com/?nid=&sid=1821553

Commission on the Intelligence Capabilities of the United States Regarding Weapons of Mass Destruction, *Report to the President of the United States*, Washington, D.C.: U.S. Government Printing Office, March 31, 2005. As of March 1, 2013:
http://govinfo.library.unt.edu/wmd/report/index.html

Defense Manpower Commission, *Defense Manpower: The Keystone of National Security*, Washington, D.C., 1976.

Department of the Army, *Commissioned Officer Professional Development and Career Management*, Washington, D.C., Department of the Army Pamphlet 600-3, 2007.

GAO—*See* U.S. Government Accountability Office; prior to 2004, *see* U.S. General Accounting Office.

Kennedy, Patrick F., deputy director of national intelligence for management, "Memorandum M-06-6019: IC Contractor Inventory," Washington, D.C.: Office of the Director of National Intelligence, April 12, 2006.

Manganaris, Alex G., "Workforce Retention Issues in the U.S. Intelligence Community (IC)," Washington, D.C.: Office of the Director of National Intelligence, Workforce Plans and Resources, January 2010. As of March 1, 2013:
http://www.dtic.mil/cgi-bin/GetTRDoc?AD=ADA535563

Mihm, J. Christopher, *Intelligence Reform: Human Capital Considerations Critical to 9/11 Commission's Proposed Reforms*, Washington, D.C.: U.S. Government Accountability Office, GAO-04-1084T, September 14, 2004. As of March 1, 2013:
http://www.gao.gov/new.items/d041084t.pdf

National Commission on Terrorist Attacks Upon the United States, *The 9/11 Commission Report: Final Report—Executive Summary*, July 2004. As of March 1, 2013:
http://govinfo.library.unt.edu/911/report/index.htm

Negroponte, John D., and Edward M. Wittenstein, "Urgency, Opportunity, and Frustration: Implementing the Intelligence Reform and Terrorism Prevention Act of 2004," *Yale Law and Policy Review*, Vol. 28, No. 2, June 2010, pp. 379–417.

Nunn, Sam, floor speech on the pending Defense Officer Personnel Management Act, U.S. Senate, August 10, 1976.

ODNI—*See* Office of the Director of National Intelligence.

Office of the Director of National Intelligence, *The National Intelligence Strategy of the United States of America: Transformation Through Integration and Innovation*, Washington, D.C., October 2005. As of March 1, 2013:
http://purl.access.gpo.gov/GPO/LPS65336

―――, *The US Intelligence Community's Five Year Strategic Human Capital Plan: An Annex to the US National Intelligence Strategy*, Washington, D.C., June 22, 2006. As of March 1, 2013:
http://purl.access.gpo.gov/GPO/LPS75660

―――, *United States Intelligence Community 500 Day Plan: Integration and Collaboration*, Washington, D.C., October 10, 2007. As of March 1, 2013:
http://purl.access.gpo.gov/GPO/LPS92732

―――, "Results of the Fiscal Year 2007 U.S. Intelligence Community, Inventory of Core Contractor Personnel," conference call, Washington, D.C., August 27, 2008. As of March 1, 2013:
http://www.fas.org/irp/news/2008/08/odni082708.html

―――, *Intelligence Community Core Contract Personnel*, Intelligence Community Directive 612, October 30, 2009. As of March 1, 2013:
http://www.fas.org/irp/dni/icd/icd-612.pdf

Office of Management and Budget, *Performance of Commercial Activities*, Washington, D.C., Circular A-76, May 29, 2003. As of March 4, 2013:
http://www.whitehouse.gov/omb/circulars_a076_a76_incl_tech_correction

Office of Personnel Management, "OPM's Workforce Planning Model," undated. As of March 4, 2013:
http://www.opm.gov/policy-data-oversight/human-capital-management/reference-materials/strategic-alignment/workforceplanning.pdf

OMB—*See* Office of Management and Budget.

OPM—*See* Office of Personnel Management.

Orszag, Peter R., director, Office of Management and Budget, "Managing the Multi-Sector Workforce," memorandum for the heads of departments and agencies, Washington, D.C., M-09-26, July 29, 2009. As of March 1, 2013:
http://www.whitehouse.gov/sites/default/files/omb/assets/memoranda_fy2009/m-09-26.pdf

Pourinski, Andrew, "Ask the Chief Human Capital Officer," *Federal News Radio*, 2007.

Public Law 80-253, National Security Act of 1947, July 26, 1947.

Public Law 96-513, Defense Officer Personnel Management Act of 1980, December 12, 1980. As of March 5, 2013:
http://thomas.loc.gov/cgi-bin/bdquery/z?d096:S.1918:

Public Law 99-433, Goldwater-Nichols Department of Defense Reorganization Act of 1986, October 1, 1986.

Public Law 108-458, Intelligence Reform and Terrorism Prevention Act of 2004, 108th Congress, December 17, 2004. As of March 1, 2013:
http://www.gpo.gov/fdsys/pkg/PLAW-108publ458/html/PLAW-108publ458.htm

Reagan, Ronald, "United States Intelligence Activities," Washington, D.C., Executive Order 12333, December 4, 1981. As of March 4, 2013:
http://www.archives.gov/federal-register/codification/executive-order/12333.html

Rostker, Bernard D., *I Want You! The Evolution of the All-Volunteer Force*, Santa Monica, Calif.: RAND Corporation, MG-265-RC, 2006. As of March 1, 2013:
http://www.rand.org/pubs/monographs/MG265.html

Rostker, Bernard D., Harry J. Thie, James L. Lacy, Jennifer H. Kawata, and Susanna W. Purnell, *The Defense Officer Personnel Management Act of 1980: A Retrospective Assessment*, Santa Monica, Calif.: RAND Corporation, R-4246-FMP, 1993. As of March 1, 2013:
http://www.rand.org/pubs/reports/R4246.html

Secretary of the Navy, *Officer Competitive Categories for the Active Duty List (ADL) of the Navy and Marine Corps*, Washington, D.C., Secretary of the Navy Instruction 1400.1B, January 27, 2006. As of March 1, 2013:
http://doni.daps.dla.mil/Directives/01000%20Military%20Personnel%20Support/
01-400%20Promotion%20and%20Advancement%20Programs/1400.1B.pdf

Smith, Roy C., "Personnel and Promotion Reduced to Its Simplest Terms," *Proceedings: The U.S. Naval Institute*, 1906, pp. 801–859.

Snider, Don M., "Strategy, Forces and Budgets: Dominant Influences in Executive Decision Making, Post–Cold War, 1989–91," in *U.S. Army War College Fourth Annual Strategy Conference*, Carlisle Barracks, Pa.: Strategic Studies Institute, February 1993. As of March 1, 2013:
http://www.strategicstudiesinstitute.army.mil/pubs/display.cfm?pubid=346

Thie, Harry J., Roger Allen Brown, Mark Berends, Rudolph H. Ehrenberg, Ann Flanagan, Claire M. Levy, William W. Taylor, Richard Eisenman, William Fedorochko, Clifford M. Graf II, Mark Hoyer, Paul Bracken, Norman T. O'Meara, Jerry M. Sollinger, Judith Larson, Kathy Mills, Nancy L. Rizor, Bernard D. Rostker, Glenn A. Gotz, Charles Robert Roll Jr., and Colin O. Halvorson, *Future Career Management Systems for U.S. Military Officers*, Santa Monica, Calif.: RAND Corporation, MR-470-OSD, 1994. As of March 1, 2013:
http://www.rand.org/pubs/monograph_reports/MR470.html

Under Secretary of Defense for Personnel and Readiness, *Commissioned Officer Promotion Program*, Washington, D.C., Department of Defense Instruction 1320.12, September 27, 2005. As of March 1, 2013:
http://www.dtic.mil/whs/directives/corres/pdf/132012p.pdf

U.S. General Accounting Office, *Force Structure: Issues Involving the Base Force*, Washington, D.C., GAO/NSIAD-93-65, January 1993. As of March 1, 2013:
http://www.gao.gov/products/NSIAD-93-65

U.S. Government Accountability Office, *Intelligence Community Personnel: Strategic Approach and Training Requirements Needed to Guide Joint Duty Program*, Washington, D.C., GAO-12-679, June 2012. As of March 1, 2013:
http://purl.fdlp.gov/GPO/gpo25508

U.S. Senate, *Intelligence Authorization Act for Fiscal Year 2008*, Senate Report 110-75, May 25, 2007. As of March 19, 2013:
http://www.intelligence.senate.gov/pdfs/11075.pdf

Vivian, Paul H., *Preparing the Defense Intelligence Community's Civilian Intelligence Workforce for the 21st Century*, Carlisle Barracks, Pa.: U.S. Army War College, 2003. As of March 1, 2013:
http://handle.dtic.mil/100.2/ADA415737

Waterman, Shaun, "Analysis: DNI Leverages Personnel Powers," United Press International, April 29, 2007. As of March 1, 2013:
http://www.upi.com/Business_News/Security-Industry/2007/04/19/
Analysis-DNI-leverages-personnel-powers/UPI-47411176988179/

White, J. P., response to Senator Sam Nunn's letter of August 11, 1977, Washington, D.C., 1977.

White House, "President Signs Intelligence Reform and Terrorism Prevention Act," press release, Office of the Press Secretary, Washington, D.C., December 17, 2004. As of March 1, 2013:
http://georgewbush-whitehouse.archives.gov/news/releases/2004/12/20041217-1.html

WMD Commission—*See* Commission on the Intelligence Capabilities of the United States Regarding Weapons of Mass Destruction.